Rebel without a Minivan

observations on life in the 'burbs

by Tracy Beckerman
author of the syndicated humor column
LOST IN SUBURBIA®

The essays in this book have appeared previously in some form in the following NJN Publishing newspapers: *The Independent Press, Hunterdon County Democrat, The Somerset Reporter,* and *The Warrren Reporter,* as well as some newspapers of the North Jersey Media Group.

Library of Congress Control Number: 2007943356

To Joel and Josh and Emily –
You fill my life with laughter!

Acknowledgements

Thanks so much to my talented editor at Fat Plum, Julie Long, for helping me mercilessly whip this book into shape, and my gifted copyeditor, Beth Polen, who is so much better than I am at knowing the difference between its and it's. Thanks also to Gene Robbins for taking a chance on the new girl in town, and to Mike Kelly for steadfastly supporting my column for so many years. More thanks to my NJN family – Mike, Jay Langley, and Craig Turpin, for consistently giving me room in their crowded papers and cheering me on with their tales of lost sheep and flying turkeys.

To Patty Meola, Barbara Rybolt, and everyone at the *Independent Press*, thanks for all the encouragement when I was just a one-paper gal. Thanks to Tim Bete for all his advice and for introducing me to Cold Tree Press, and to Peter Honsberger at Cold Tree for his brilliant guidance. Also, hugs to my friend Suzette Martinez Standring for her wit, wisdom, and our shared distaste for tankinis.

So much gratitude to my friends and family for all their support, especially my parents, Harvey and Carol Baron; my in-laws, Steve and Nancy Beckerman; and all my sibs and sibs-in-law! And of course, my eternal gratitude to my husband, Joel, for his never-ending love and encouragement, and belief in me from the beginning!

Table of Contents

Rebel without a Minivan

observations on life in the 'burbs

Introduction

There was never any doubt in my mind that I would always be a city girl. I worked in the television industry, which clearly made me hip and cool, and needless to say, hip, cool people do not live in the suburbs. Women who drive minivans and men with comb-overs — they live in the suburbs. I clung to my convictions until I was seven months pregnant with my first child. Finally I realized there wasn't a chance in hell I'd be able to get a Peg Perego stroller up a four-flight walk-up every day (although it might be a good way to work off the weight I'd gained without resorting to liposuction). Then I thought about rigging a pulley system through the window so I wouldn't have to give up my rent-controlled brownstone duplex, but my husband pulled the plug on that idea.

So, ten months later, we moved to the suburbs of New Jersey. My eight-month-old son, the city baby, cried the first time I put him down on a patch of grass. And though he had endured earsplitting city noise, he was unable to sleep through the sonic boom of all the lawn mowers going at 6:30 in the morning. Eventually he adjusted to both the grass and the mowers. I, however, dug my heels into those well-manicured lawns until my neighbors and I were able to reach something of an understanding: They agreed to accept my short, spiky hair, my inability to get my children's socks their whitest white, and my refusal to wear makeup to go to the mall; I agreed to stop laughing out loud when they discussed household cleaning products, 101 uses for ground beef, and being kept awake at night by the sound of woodchucks mating in their backyard.

Obviously, no self-respecting city girl ever thinks, "Gee, when I grow up, I want to live in the suburbs." It's just one of those things that happens, like taxes and varicose veins. One day you're running off to sample sales… the next day, garage sales.

For some people, it's a seamless transition. "Okay kids, pile in the minivan; after soccer practice, we're going out for a Happy Meal!" Wahoo!

For me, it was more like going through a car wash without a car.

And it wasn't just the suburb thing. It was the whole "married mother of two and a dog who moved to the suburbs" thing. I wondered: How did I get here? Where did all this cellulite come from? Who are these two children, and why do they keep calling me mommy?

These are the questions that kept me awake at night (that, and the aforementioned two children yelling for drinks of water). I figured the only way I could get any sleep was to put a watercooler in the hallway and start writing a column for the local paper.

On the upside, it's been a great way to get my ya-yas out. Like, when someone tries to sneak twelve items into the ten-items-or-less checkout line ahead of me, I can rat them out to 90,000 of their neighbors. Of course, on the flip side, when I experience something deeply personal and then have the stupidity to put it in print, the whole world knows about it — or, at least, my little corner does.

For example, one morning I went to get my coffee at Dunkin' Donuts.

Me: "Can I get a medium hazelnut, please?"

Coffee guy: "With sugar or without?"

Me: "Without."

Coffee guy: "Okay. And by the way, how did your boob job turn out?"

See what I mean?

What I didn't expect, however, were the cheers from so many other moms on the playground. Although many of them looked the part of the typical suburban housewife, internally they fought many of the same demons I did. Who would have thought that "Mall Mom," in her Donna Karan twin set and her mighty Town and Country minivan with the DVD entertainment system, also bore a secret tattoo on her butt from the day she turned 35 and was feeling old and defiant?

But could these moms relate to my suburban-induced angst? My ordeals in child-rearing? My husband's inability to multitask? My seasonal woes and body-image neuroses? Apparently so. On the same school playground one day, a mom I'd never met before walked by with a double jogging stroller occupied by two drooling toddlers, leaned in, and whispered to me, "I sneak french fries, too!" If I hadn't just written a column about my affair with french fries, I probably would have thought this lady had lost her well-coiffed marbles. But instead I grinned. We are *all* sisters in suburbia. Misunderstood moms. Rebels, with or without a minivan.

Prologue:
Do You Have a License for That Outfit?

"Hello?"

"Yes, ma'am, I'm looking for Tracy Beckerman."

"This is Ms. Beckerman."

"Ms. Beckerman, this is the fashion police. We received a call about a possible six-one-seven at the mall."

"What's a six-one-seven?"

"That would be a hot-weather-wear violation. Ms. Beckerman, could you tell me what you were wearing on July 23rd at approximately 11 a.m.?"

"That was the day it was 96 degrees out, right? Um, I was wearing a sleeveless t-shirt and shorts, I think."

"Yes, ma'am. That outfit was not designer clothing, was it, Ms. Beckerman?"

"No. Old Navy, I think."

"I see. And were you or were you not wearing sandals that exposed the chipped nail polish on your toes at that time?"

"Well, uh, we just got back from vacation with the kids and I haven't had time to go get a pedicure yet, officer."

"Uh-huh. And is it also true that you were not wearing any makeup OR jewelry on your trip to the mall, Ms. Beckerman?"

"I, er, it was just so hot out... the makeup would have melted as soon as I put it on! Besides, I have a tan, officer.

I don't really need makeup."

"Everyone needs makeup, ma'am. Especially at the mall. I'm afraid I'm going to have to cite you for reckless dressing and failure to properly accessorize."

"Isn't that a little harsh, officer? I mean, it was unbearably hot out."

"Ms. Beckerman, the weather is no excuse for committing a fashion violation. If we let you off, we'd have to let off all the women wearing last year's DKNY and too-tight Marc Jacobs jeans. What kind of example would that set for our impressionable, fashion-conscious youth?"

"I understand, officer. But I am getting a paraffin pedicure and a bikini wax tomorrow, and I did spend $500 on a new Theory suit while I was at the mall."

"That's no excuse for breaking the law, ma'am."

"Hmm. Hey officer, I just got my husband a terrific Hugo Boss shirt that's too big for him. What's your neck size?"

"Are you trying to bribe a fashion police officer, ma'am?"

"Oh no, sir. It's just that this is my third violation and last time my husband said if I got one more, he was going to cut up my GAP credit card."

"Tell it to the judge, lady."

Welcome to My World

Reality Bites

At eight years old, my son is fairly certain that the Tooth Fairy doesn't exist. However, he won't admit it publicly for fear that he'll lose out on a pretty profitable deal. As far as I'm concerned, this wouldn't necessarily be a bad thing, because the Tooth Fairy is feeling a little financially strapped these days.

You see, she herself has tooth problems. While my children are busy yanking out their loose teeth like junior dentists, I've been busy trying to save mine. And while the going rate for their teeth is about two bucks, it looks like mine will run me a slightly steeper $400 a tooth.

Yes, age has caught up with me, although not exactly where I expected it. Sun damage, gray hairs... I was prepared for all that. But aging gums? I didn't remember reading about that one in the Over-35 handbook.

My first indication that there was a problem was a spoonful of ice cream that sent such a shot of pain through my mouth, it made me reminisce about childbirth. I thought I had a cavity or maybe lost a filling, but no.

"Your gums are receding," declared the periodontist. And here I thought only hairlines receded.

"And this is bad because..." I wondered.

"It exposes your nerves, which is why you're having pain," he said slowly, as though I were a foreigner or an idiot.

He droned on for a bit about how we need that gum tissue to hold our teeth in and protect them from invading bacteria. And then he laid out a laundry list of all the horrible things I'd done to create the problem: over-brushing, grinding, eating sugar, and smoking. Honestly, I felt like Charlie Brown when Lucy lists his myriad of faults. Loser with a Capital L branded on my forehead. She Who Doesn't Take Care of Her Teeth. Gumzilla.

"And of course, genetics plays a part, too," he summed up.

Thank God. At least I could blame one thing on someone else.

The worst news was not the state of my mouth or the potential pain involved in repairing the damage, but the cost for this dental insult: Ten teeth at the aforementioned $400 a tooth.

Now I'm no mathematician, but even I knew that added up to the big screen TV I now would not be getting.

I left the surgeon's office and started making phone calls. First I gave my husband the bad news. Then I called our insurance carrier to find out about our coverage. I whined to a couple of friends. And lastly I called my mother to blame my father's genes.

Meanwhile, back at Tooth Fairy Central, there was a message on my answering machine from the orthodontist regarding our consultation for my son's corrective mouth wear.

"Can you tell me again how much that will be?" I asked when I called back to confirm the appointment.

"Fifteen hundred dollars," she said without batting an eyelash. Truthfully, I couldn't see her because we were on the phone, but I just know she didn't bat an eyelash.

"And that doesn't include future orthodonture work, right?" I asked miserably.

"That's correct," she said.

And so I sat down to begin filling out a multitude of dental insurance pre-authorization forms, knowing they would be denied because all of the work was elective. As I went through this exercise in insurance futility, my son appeared at the door.

"Guess what?" he said excitedly. "I pulled out my loose tooth!" He showed me the evidence in his hand and the gaping hole in his mouth. "I guess I'll be getting a visit from the Tooth Fairy tonight, huh?"

Sorry, kid. I think the Tooth Fairy filed for Chapter 11.

Lifestyles of the Not-So-Rich and Unknown

There are people who know famous people, and there are people who know people who know famous people. I'm in the second category.

I have actually met some famous people on my own, but I can't really call anybody who's famous a friend or even an acquaintance. Although I like to think I make a memorable first impression, I'm pretty sure if my name were mentioned to the celebrities I've met, they would respond with a blank look and a resounding "Tracy who?"

My brother is one of those people who actually knows famous people, and they in turn know him. This is due to the fact that he is their doctor, which means, unfortunately, that he is ethically bound not to share any information about them. To me, this is like owning a chocolate factory and being on a diet. Although he doesn't seem to mind, I feel bad for him because everyone knows how cool it is to talk about famous people when you know them personally. Of course, he could tell me and then *I* could talk about them, which is probably still unethical, especially since I'm a journalist, but who would be the wiser? The problem with this is that everyone *also* knows that it's very pathetic to talk about celebrities as *though* you know them, but only actually know *about* them through someone else, twice removed. With that kind of association, you might as well admit you read about them in *People* magazine.

Still, he knows we all know he knows famous people and that it drives us crazy that he won't talk about them. Maybe that's better than saying anything at all.

Me: "So who are you treating these days?"

My brother: "You know I can't tell you that."

Me: "Is it someone famous? Did she just have a baby? Did she just have liposuction???"

Him: "I can't tell you that."

Me: "She did, didn't she?"

Him: "I didn't say that."

Me: "Wait until I tell everyone about this!"

Him: "I DIDN'T SAY THAT!!!"

Really though, the beauty of knowing famous people is it makes you something of a celebrity yourself. Through your cool celebrity friends, you can go backstage at rock concerts, attend exclusive openings, and even go to the Oscars, although you will sit so far away from the actual celebrities that you won't know whether it's Brad or Angelina on the stage. Because he knows famous people, my brother gets many of the perks of being rich and famous, without being famous or, unfortunately, rich.

In our celebrity-obsessed culture, it's understandable that we all want to bask in the glow of famous people. They make lots of money, get into the best restaurants, and get to name their children after fruits and vegetables. But I honestly wouldn't want to live my life in the limelight just so I could get a great table at a new restaurant only to worry that the paparazzi were stalking me for shots of the cellulite on my thighs. Then I would go to the supermarket and see close-ups of my cellulite splashed on the cover of some trashy magazine, and the person in line behind me would look at the cover and then at the Häagen-Dazs in my cart, and give me a knowing look.

Then, of course, since I was a celebrity, I would have to go to a doctor for liposuction.

And then I would hope and pray…

…that my doctor didn't tell his sister about it.

Putting the "P" in "Pool"

When we were looking for a house, a pool in the backyard was certainly not at the top of our list of priorities. It actually fell somewhere between being on a quiet street and having four toilets. However, when we did find our house and learned it had a pool, we decided to buy it anyway. Although the house only had three toilets, we figured the kids would probably end up peeing in the pool often enough that the toilet issue would be a draw.

There were, of course, a number of concerns we had with this unexpected acquisition. First of all, having small children, I was worried about the safety issues. So we put up a big fence, got the kids some swim lessons, laid down the pool law, and assured them that we would never, ever go to McDonald's again if anyone went in the pool area without an adult.

Unfortunately, despite all our precautions, we did have some casualties.

There was the frog, normally considered a good swimmer, who drowned in the shallow end. The field mouse, which met the same untimely demise. And a squirrel who went bobbing for the crab apples that had fallen from the tree behind the pool and never bobbed back up.

Now, I am quite the animal lover, and I did not take these losses of lives lightly. As the person who turns the pool filter on each morning, I am also the one who usually discovers the soggy surprises. I react with appropriate sadness, shock, and dismay, which usually sounds something like, *"Ewww, there's a dead thing in the pool!!!"* To which my husband responds, "That's what happens when you have a pool."

Yes, we were somewhat prepared for the "ick" factor, as I call it, which also includes worms after a big rain, bugs doing the backstroke, and the occasional aforementioned toilet mishap of varying degrees of ickiness. What I was not prepared for was the lack of pool etiquette from some of our swim guests. This is where some folks could take a couple of hints from Miss Pool Manners.

I have become accustomed to guests coming without their own towels and sunscreen, children who need water wings but don't bring them, and people who are happy to snack and drink all day without offering to help refill the kitty. It would seem, I told my husband, that this was not our family pool, but a beach club.

There was the child who showed up without a swimsuit for a swim date with my son. "My mom said I could borrow one," he told me. They don't even provide that service at the local swim club, thank you very much.

Then there was the friend who told me that rather than spend the money to join her local pool, she would just bring her kids over to swim at our house this summer.

Don't get me wrong, I love to have people over to enjoy

the pool with us. My point is that an invitation to someone's pool is just that: an invitation. It carries with it all the same gestures of thoughtful gratitude as an invitation to someone's home: Bring your own stuff. Offer to bring food or drink (although expect to be turned down—remember, it's the gesture that counts). Don't overstay your welcome, and please:

Don't pee in the pool.

Cinema Suburbisimo

I love going to the movies. I love the popcorn, the enormous sodas, the surround sound—the whole experience. Okay, maybe not the gummy bears on the floor, but the rest of it is great. However, the effort involved in going to the movies in New York City is enough to send even the most die-hard fan panting and screaming straight to Blockbuster.

A typical outing would go something like this: You order your tickets over the phone and pay a two-dollar surcharge per ticket because if you actually went to the box office, the movie would invariably be sold out unless you arrived two hours in advance, and even so, it might still be sold out. But buying tickets over the phone guarantees you nothing except a seat in the front row looking up at the top of your eyeballs unless you arrive an hour early to wait in the ticketholders' line to actually get into the movie.

Still with me?

Then there's the cost: $18 for the tickets, $20 for the snacks, and another $5 for a second bucket of popcorn to replace the one you accidentally dumped on the floor, for a grand total of $43.

Sounds like a fun way to spend the evening, huh?

Having lived in Manhattan my whole adult life, I had

no idea that this was a city thing until my husband and I moved out to the suburbs. For our first movie, we bought our tickets in advance, wolfed down some greasy pizza at a time when only retirees in Florida would eat, and arrived at the theater an hour before showtime to find it... closed. Neither of us could understand this. We figured that maybe in the suburbs they didn't open the doors until 45 minutes before the film, so we started a ticketholders' line.

We were so proud of ourselves. Even on our best New York City movie date, we had never been first in line.

So there we were, standing on the sidewalk grinning like idiots for half an hour, completely alone, until the door to the theater opened and an employee came out.

"Can I help you?" he asked.

"We're just waiting for the movie," we said. "We started a ticketholders' line." We held up our two-dollar-surcharged prizes.

"It doesn't start for half an hour," he said.

"We know," we said cheerfully. "We just wanted to get a good seat. When will you be letting people in?"

"Uh, about ten minutes before the movie starts," he said, and went back inside. We still didn't get it and waited in our own line, alone, another twenty minutes until the doors opened. We raced in to get the perfect seats, ran to get snacks, and hightailed it to the bathrooms, lest we lose our prized location. And then, at about five minutes before the movie started, the other people started trickling in. Not running. Not elbowing other people out of the way. Just strolling in. By the time the previews started, the theater was full, and we were exhausted.

We kept up this idiocy for about six months before we finally got the point that things happen at a slower pace in the 'burbs.

That was about seven years ago, and I have to admit, over time, we'd gotten somewhat complacent about the whole movie thing.

Fast-forward to this summer. It was a Saturday night, we had a babysitter, and we decided to go see a new block-buster, opening weekend.

We went for a leisurely dinner and then headed to the theater about 15 minutes before showtime to find… a ticketholders' line winding its way completely around the inside perimeter of the theater, out the door, and into the parking lot.

"Even if there are any tickets left, we're going to end up watching the movie at the top of our eyeballs," I said to my husband.

I thought about running out to rent some wheelchairs so we could move to the front of the line, but this looked like an angry crowd and I was afraid of becoming yet another movie theater-riot statistic.

"When did the suburbs get to be so, uh, urban?" I asked him.

"Must have been during those four years we didn't go out because we had little kids and sleep deprivation," he said.

"We could buy tickets now for the next showing and go get some coffee or something," I said glumly.

My husband grimaced. It wasn't that he didn't delight in the idea of spending two and a half hours talking to me, but we both knew that if we went to the next showing, we'd be late getting our babysitter home. And then we'd only get about six hours of sleep because our well-rested children would be clamoring for breakfast at some ungodly hour.

So we decided to go home. On the way, we stopped at Blockbuster and picked up something we'd both already seen because all the new releases were already rented. Then we made some popcorn, turned on the flick, and promptly fell asleep on the couch.

It may not have been the most exciting theater experience. But it only cost us $4.95 — and we didn't have to peel gummy bears off the soles of our shoes.

Beware of Moms Shopping for School Supplies

If you go shopping for fall school supplies early — like, say, July — chances are you can get everything you need in one fell swoop and it will be a pretty uneventful outing. But wait until the last minute, like the week before school starts, and not only will you be freaking out because the store shelves are empty, you might also find yourself the victim of school-supply rage.

It's not that I *wanted* to wait until the last minute, but I had only just gotten the lists from my kids' teachers the day before school began. Clearly, the teachers had no idea what a strain this put on us moms. Do the kids care if they have the black-and-white composition notebooks with string binding demanded by their teachers? No, of course not. All they care about is that you get them this year's must-have sneakers so they don't get laughed off the playground. But moms want to get off on the right foot with the new teachers, so, school supply list in one hand and whining children in the other, off they go to hunt for protractors and be ignored by salespeople.

Those black-and-white composition notebooks must have been a hot ticket item this year, because try as I might, I could not find the darn things. I knew the store carried them because there were brightly colored posters of school supplies including these particular notebooks. But after half an hour of searching, I found only one lone composition notebook partially buried beneath some Spider-Man folders.

While I looked around in vain for a salesperson to harass, another mother approached me.

"Where did you find that?" she asked accusingly.

"Over there," I said, pointing to the Spider-Man shelf. "But I don't think that's where they belong, and I'm pretty sure there aren't any more."

"So you're telling me that's the last one?" she said, hands on her hips. "You're holding the very last black-and-white composition notebook in this store?"

I couldn't decide if this woman was a member of the school-supply police and was placing me under arrest for wanton notebook-hoarding, or if she was just nuts.

Either way, she had me blocked with her shopping cart against the Dora the Explorer notebooks, and I had no escape.

"Well, I don't know for a fact that this is the last one," I said, trying to look innocent. "Why don't you find a salesperson and ask them?"

"There *are* no salespeople," she hissed, as though this were my doing. "And I need four of those notebooks."

I decided she was indeed nuttier than Mr. Peanut, and figured the only way to get out of this confrontation unscathed was to lie.

"There are more school supplies down there by gift

wrap," I said, pointing to the other end of the store. "I haven't checked there yet, but if you want to..."

As Crazy School-Supply Lady grabbed her cart and took off to find the mythical notebooks, I grabbed my cart and ran to the checkout lines before she could realize she'd been duped.

"Did you find everything okay?" asked the checkout girl. It's a standard question. You're supposed to say yes, and then they smile and ring you up.

"Well, actually, I couldn't find more of these composition notebooks," I said, holding up the world's last one. "And there were no salespeople around to help, and then this crazy lady accosted me in the school-supply aisle because she needed these too and thought I'd conspired to take the last one, and she was really scary and I have to get out of here fast before she realizes I sent her to the wrong place to look for more."

The checkout girl looked at me nervously. Clearly they hadn't covered this in checkout school.

Just then, I felt a tap on my shoulder. The woman in line behind me — who had no school supplies in her cart and therefore appeared to be in her right mind — leaned forward.

"I think they have more of those notebooks at the drugstore in town," she said.

"Really?" I asked desperately. She nodded.

"Thank you so much," I said. "This has been a nightmare."

She smiled. "I know. I did it yesterday."

I'm Just Looking

Although I am a big fan of shopping at local businesses, I usually go out of my way *not* to shop at my local drugstore. It really has nothing to do with the store itself, or the people who work there. It is actually a really nice store. The problem is, everyone I know shops there. So if I go there to pick up anything from wart remover to a pregnancy test, my private business will surely get around faster than if it were published in the newspaper.

Welcome to life in a small town. My neighbor and my daughter's teacher stand next to me in the hair-color aisle as we all try to find our "natural" shades. My mailman hovers over me as I peruse the extra-strength antiperspirants. My babysitter and I discover we use the same brand of tampons. And the whole world seems to be shopping the day I need treatment for a yeast infection.

Yes, I know that everyone else has to deal with the same embarrassing issues that I do. I would just rather they didn't know that I know that they know about all my stuff. And vice versa.

Of course when it comes to things like warts and antiperspirant, there's always the question as to whom it's really for. Is it for me, my husband, or the kids? Unfortunately, it seems all the really mortifying stuff is just for us ladies, and often there is no doubt that the shopper and the user are the same.

Now, having someone you know nearby when you are shopping for personal items is one thing. Worse is when that person sees you comparing treatments of something you don't really want to discuss with *anybody*, and they decide the neighborly thing is to offer you advice.

Nosy Neighbor: "Hi!"

Me: "Oh… hi."

NN: "Hmmm. You know, I still think those five-day treatments work better than the single-dose ones."

Me: "Okay…"

NN: "Of course, you have to put up with the icky mess for a while, but then at least you know the yeast infection is really gone."

Me: "Okay…"

NN: "Of course, if you have a really bad one, you might want to go with the seven-day cream."

Me: "AAAAUUUUUGGGHHHHHH!"

At this point I will usually bluff and say I'm just looking for next time, I'm actually here to pick up some photos, and then I will dash to the front and pick up some photos which I always have ready for just such an emergency, and then I will get in my car and drive fifty miles to another drugstore and buy some cream for my yeast infection and then go back home and smother my face with a pillow.

Finally, many hours and much chocolate later, I am recovered from my ordeal.

"How was your day?" asks my husband when he gets home.

"Okay. How was yours?"

"Fine," he says. "Oh, could you do me a favor tomorrow?"

"What?"

"Could you pick me up something at the drugstore?"

Interlude I:
Overheard at the Beckerman Dinner Table

"What's this stuff?"

"That's meatloaf."

"Ewww. I don't like it."

"How do you know? You haven't even tried it yet."

"I can tell."

"How can you tell?"

"Because it's brown and it smells funny."

"It doesn't smell funny. It's just like hamburger. You like hamburger."

"It doesn't look like hamburger."

"Here, try it with some ketchup."

"Can I put the ketchup on my mashed potatoes?"

(Sigh.) "If you want."

"How come there are bumpy things in my mashed potatoes?"

"Because they're homemade."

"I don't like bumpy things. I like it smooth."

"It tastes the same."

"*No.* The bumpy things don't feel good in my mouth."

"Here. I'll scoop the bumpy things out."

"Do I have to eat the broccoli?"

"Yes."

"Why?"

"Because green things make you grow."

"Can't I just eat my boogers instead?"

"Ugh. That's disgusting. No, boogers don't count."

"How come?"

"Because they don't have the same vitamins in them."

"Can't I just take my chewable vitamins instead?"

"No. If you want to qualify for dessert, you have to eat some broccoli."

"What's for dessert?"

"Fruit."

"That's not dessert. Dessert is supposed to be junky."

"Well, tonight dessert is fruit."

"If we're having fruit for dessert, then I'm not going to eat the broccoli."

"Do what you want."

"Fine! I will!" (Pause.) "Look mom, I ate all my broccoli!"

"No, you didn't. You threw it on the floor and the dog ate it."

"I didn't. It fell when I was scooping it into my mouth."

"*Every* piece fell when you scooped it into your mouth?"

"Yeah."

"But none of the mashed potatoes fell, right?"

"That stuff stuck to my fork better."

"I'll get you some more broccoli."

"No, that's okay. I'm full and Daddy says I don't have to

eat any more when I'm full, so I'll just have dessert now."

"You're too full for dinner but you have room for dessert?"

"Yeah, dessert goes into a different part of my stomach where there's more room."

"Is that so?"

"Yup. Hey mom, what are *you* eating?"

"TUMS."

Who Are These Children and Why Are They Calling Me Mommy?

If I'm Asleep, I Must Be Dreaming

There is nothing more precious to me than my children.

Except maybe a good night's sleep.

The last time I slept well — that is, for more than four hours at a time — was probably around the same time I still fit into my size-eight jeans. That would be before my first child was born.

You remember those days. Staying out late. Sleeping in the next day. And when you got tired from all that sleeping, you took a nap. I look back on that time with nostalgia and longing. Do I miss the staying out late, the lack of responsibility, the one-on-one time I had with my husband?

Nah. It's the deep, personal relationship I had with my *pillow* that I miss desperately!

Now I have small children, so it's a given that I'm not supposed to get much in the way of solid sleep. And I was prepared for the three-a.m. feedings in the first year. I got used to the requests for a drink of water in the third year. I anticipated contending with some monsters under my son's bed in the fifth year. But I figured at some point, they'd stop waking in the middle of the night and maybe, *maybe*, even sleep past 5:30 in the morning, too.

Ha!

So there I am one night, examining the insides of my eyelids in a blissful, unconscious, dead-to-the-world kind of way, when a familiar wail rouses me.

"Mommy. Mommy." I look at the clock. 2:55 a.m.

"Mommy!" Again. A little louder.

"It's for you," my husband says with his eyes closed as he rolls over.

This is the part that always amazes me. This is the man who always says, "I want us to be equals in our marriage. Equal partners. Equal parents." Yeah. Sure. Right. Until it's three a.m. and one of the kids wakes up. Then all of a sudden "equal" goes right out the window and it's every sleeping man and woman for themselves.

I stumble out of bed, down the hall, into my son's room. He's sitting up in bed, wide awake.

"What is it, what's the matter?" I expect maybe a bad dream or a stomachache.

"What are we going to do tomorrow?" he asks.

"We're going to take a nap," I tell him as I tuck him back in.

"Why are we going to take a nap?"

"Because we're going to be very tired from getting up in the middle of the night," I say. "Go back to sleep."

Half an hour later it happens again.

"Mommy. Mommy!"

Why does he always call *me*? I don't get it. His first word was "Dada." When he gets banged up, he cries for his daddy. Yet when he wakes up at some ungodly hour in the middle of the night, I'm the one he calls.

I stare at my husband. He's playing chicken. I know he's awake and he *knows* I know he's awake, but his eyes are still closed, which means I lose. I give the sheet a good yank as I get out of bed. Now he has to lie there and be cold if he wants to be convincing as a real sleeping person.

The next morning my son is bouncing off the walls as usual, full of pep, energy, and Fruit Loops. My husband looks pretty well rested, too. I, however, feel like someone rubbed a Brillo pad under my eyelids.

"Well, that was a drag last night," my husband tells me.

Uh-huh. Which part would that be, honey? The part when you woke up, rolled over, and went back to sleep, or the part when you woke up, pretended to be asleep, and then went back to sleep?

The next day I consult my mom friends, *my* mother, and the bible for tired parents, *How to Solve Your Child's Sleep Problems*, by Dr. Richard Ferber. Everybody has a different opinion. I decide to just wing it.

That night as I'm putting the kids to sleep, I read them a book, sing them a song, and whisper a little something in their ears.

At 2:55 a.m., I hear a distant cry from down the hall. "Daddy!"

Eyes closed, I smile and elbow my husband. "It's for you."

TV or Not TV (That Is the Question)

After asking, bribing, and finally threatening my son, I said, "If you don't put away your toys, there will be no TV." I was prepared for a tantrum or compliance; both have been known to happen. Instead, he held up his pointer fingers and thumbs to form the letter "W," and replied, "Whatever."

Excuse me, but at what point did my seven-year-old son become a teenager?

A little later, I informed my five-year-old daughter that it was bedtime.

"Who's gonna make me?" she demanded.

"I am," I responded.

"Yeah, you and what army?" she asked. I was dumb-founded. These are not phrases I routinely use around the house. Nor did I believe my children had learned these things from their teachers in school (at least I hoped not).

I knew from consulting my library of child development resources that it is common for kids this age to rebel in order to separate from their parents and solidify their individuality. But it is *not* common for them to tell me to "stuff a sock in it."

I thought perhaps my son might be picking up these phrases from his classmates with older siblings, and my daughter picking them up from my son. So I called some of the other moms to check this out, but they were experiencing the same thing as me. Here we had a generation of rude children, and no idea how they got that way.

Then one morning, I was making school lunches in the kitchen while the kids watched a cartoon on TV.

Suddenly my ears perked up as I heard the mother say to the teenage daughter, "Debbie, you have to stay here and watch your little sister."

Then I heard Debbie respond, "Whatever." I didn't have to see the TV screen to know she was holding up her pointer fingers and thumbs to make a "W."

Aha! Now I knew the source. But what was the solution? Toss the TVs? It wouldn't matter. Between the fast-food toys and the TV show action figures at Toys "R" Us, the commercialization of my children was all around. I was outnumbered.

The solution, I realized, was not to shut out all of the commercial input, but to temper it with good old-fashioned parental counter-input.

I took my son aside. "Do you think some of the things Debbie says on TV are nice things, or not-so-nice things?"

He thought for a minute. "Not-so-nice things," he responded.

"Do you think it hurts people's feelings when somebody says not-so-nice things to them?"

My son looked at me solemnly and said, amazingly,

"Yes. And feelings are very fragile things. They can break. Just like bones."

I smiled. He gets it, I thought.

I looked at this little boy who seemed to understand more about the ways of the world than some of our nation's leaders, and I felt a surge of love… and respect.

"Sweetie," I said to him, "I want you to try to think before you say something that's not-so-nice to someone, if it might make them feel bad, okay?"

He looked at me innocently and said, "Whatever."

You Never Forget Your First

My daughter is in love.

While this concept may strike fear in the hearts of most parents, I am unconcerned because the object of her affection is a pink blanket called, of course, Blankie. That's what my daughter calls it. I call it something less endearing: "that horrible pink thing," or the more specific "Skanky Blankie." It used to be pink, but now it's more the color of Silly Putty, riddled with holes and hanging threads, and permanently discolored in the corners where she's sucked the life out of it.

For her, Blankie is *it:* Undemanding, unconditional, pure comfort. When Blankie is around, life is good. When Blankie is in the wash or, God forbid, missing, life has no meaning, no purpose. It's been this way for six whole years with no end in sight. And much as my husband and I would like to deep-six Blankie, we know that she needs it. We just hope it won't go to college with her.

The funny thing about my daughter's attachment to Blankie is that it's totally incongruous with the child she is the rest of the time. I joke to my friends that she is six going on sixteen. She tells my son he can't watch a certain show on TV because "it's inappropriate for children his age."

When she runs into a friend at the park, she asks, "What brings you here?" And when my husband is speaking too loudly on the phone, she asks him to keep it down because "it's really quite distracting to her." (Distracting from what? Watching TV, of course.)

She sings along with Sheryl Crow on her CD player, wears funky clothes, and tries to escape from the house with lipstick on. And when I tell her we're going to Starbucks for Frappuccinos, she says, "Right on, Mom!"

I have no idea where she gets all this.

My husband laughs. "She's just like you. Don't you see it?"

"I don't have a Skanky Blankie," I point out. He rolls his eyes.

Still, she does have her six-year-old moments: temper tantrums, crying jags, and refusals to cooperate. But I have days like that, too, so maybe she's just in training to be a 38-year-old mother of two.

Anyway, one night the unthinkable happened. I handed her Blankie at bedtime. She brought it in for a snuggle, and then made a face.

"I don't want this. I want Blankie's sister." (That would be the brand-new, barely touched blankie we kept in the drawer in case of emergency).

"What?" I said in disbelief. "Why?"

"This one smells bad," she said matter-of-factly. "And it has too many holes." I had to agree with her on that one. So I took away the old blankie and gave her the new one.

The next morning she came downstairs with New

Blankie in her arms.

"So, are we done with Old Blankie?" I asked her.

"Yes," she said.

"Well, what should we do with the old one?" I figured a ceremony and proper burial, maybe. Or perhaps a mercy killing.

"Well…" She thought for a minute. "I guess you can throw it in the trash. Or maybe keep it as a souvenir of my childhood."

Right on, sweetie!

Let's Talk about Sex

I don't know too many parents who would tell their kids where babies come from before their kids actually ask, present company included. Ask me about religion, death, the existence of tooth fairies, I'm a regular encyclopedia of parental knowledge. But ask me about sex, and suddenly I clam up. Not that I don't know about it. I do have two kids, after all. But explaining it in technical terms to my kids — well, that's about as high on my list of favorite activities as cleaning the toilet bowl.

Somehow, much to my relief, I made it to my children's sixth and eighth years without having to deal with that topic. And then one day as I was carpooling three second-graders and my six-year-old daughter home from school, my son announced that someone had said a bad word at recess that day.

"What's the word?" I asked him.

"S-E-X," he spelled. I jerked the car over to avoid hitting a tree.

"What's that spell?" asked my daughter.

"Sex! It spells *sex!*" yelled one of the other kids in the car. "And it's *horrible.*"

"It's not horrible and it's not a bad word," I said, trying

to maintain my composure lest I alert the kids that we were in dangerous parenting territory by accidentally running over someone's cat. I wondered why these things always came up when my husband was away on a business trip.

I took a deep, cleansing breath. "Does anyone know what it is?" I asked. The three older kids all said yes. That two of them knew didn't surprise me. One of them was something of a junior scientist and the other watched MTV. That my son knew, however, absolutely floored me. I knew I hadn't told him and his father hadn't told him, so unless they had started teaching that particular lesson on *Rugrats*, I didn't have a clue how he found out.

"What do you think it is?" I asked my son.

He explained it. Suffice it to say, he was mostly right... except for the part about something getting "stuck."

Aside from this minor correction, I was saved the trouble of having to delve into the actual nuts and bolts of sex. And I was more than happy to change the subject and ignore my daughter yelling from the backseat, "Wait, I don't understand. The man does what???" until my son said, "But why do people do that?"

"To make babies," said his friend, the junior scientist and designated human sexuality expert.

My son grimaced. "Is that the *only* way?" he asked with a shudder.

"No," said the expert. "They can mix parts of the man and woman in a dish and then when the cells join together, they put it in the mother to grow into a baby." I was impressed. But I imagined my son picturing a man's leg and a woman's elbow being stirred in a soup bowl.

"I think that's how I was made," announced my son.

I snorted. "Why do you think that?"

"Because you and dad wouldn't do that *other* thing," he said with certainty.

"Surprise!"

He suddenly looked exhausted, as though the weight of this knowledge was too much for his little eight-year-old mind to bear. Actually, it was almost too much for my 38-year-old mind to bear. Fortunately we had arrived at our destination, and I was able to suggest that we table the conversation for another time.

Later that night, after I put my daughter to bed, I sat my son down and explained about the birds and the bees, and why sex isn't so horrible when you're an adult and you love someone and want to have a baby.

I answered all his questions, and when he didn't have any more, I tucked him in and kissed him goodnight.

As I walked down the hall, relieved that this day was finally over, I heard my daughter call from her bedroom.

"Mommy, Mommy. Where do babies come from?"

I sighed. "The stork brings them."

"Is that after the storks have sex?"

I'm Not as Think as You Dumb I Am

I used to be the smartest woman in the world. I know this may be kind of presumptuous to say (not to mention arrogant), but it's true. Until recently, my kids thought that I was absolutely brilliant. I could add double-digit numbers in my head (oooh...), I could name all the oceans and continents (ahhh...), and I knew all the colors of the rainbow. Then my kids started school, and slowly my stronghold on brilliance started to ebb away. By the time my son hit fourth grade, I had become an absolute moron.

Somehow I had made it through primary school, high school, and college, getting good grades to boot, so I must have learned something. But sometime between my graduation from Penn State and now, all those little facts I swore I'd never use (and actually never did) have either disappeared into the recesses of my mind, or were part of the brain cells that were destroyed when I gave birth to my children.

Much as I hate to support the gender stereotype, I was never that interested in (or particularly good at) math and science. But now I have a husband and a son who excel at both, which would normally be a good thing because my

husband could theoretically help the kids with their homework and we'd all be happy. The problem is, my husband
is never home at homework time, which leaves only me to
answer the question: Is a rhombus a parallelogram?

"Is this a trick question?" I asked my son.

"No," he said. "It's a homework question."

"Isn't a rhombus a kind of Spanish dance?" I asked.

"No. That's a rumba."

"Oh. What's a rhombus?"

"It's kind of like a square except it's slanted," he responded, disgust thinly veiled.

"Oh. What's a parallelogram?"

"Two pairs of parallel sides," he said.

"Hmmm. You know, I happen to know for a fact that
this is one of those things you'll never use in your adult life."

"That's fine, Mom, but I will have to use it in my
childhood to pass fourth-grade math."

"I mean, when Dad bought me an engagement ring, he
didn't ask me if I wanted a rhombus-shaped diamond..."

"Mom..."

"Or when we renovate the house, the architect is not
going to ask me if I want a rhombus-shaped bedroom..."

"Mom!"

"Okay. Let's see... I know," I finally said triumphantly.
"Let's call Dad!"

I dialed. "Hey honey, I have a question for you. Is a
rhombus a parallelogram?"

"Yes," he said, and hung up.

That was it. Just yes. He knew, he answered, he hung

up. I, on the other hand, had worked up such a mental sweat that my eyebrows hurt.

Now, I have never claimed to be a genius at math. But still, it's a little embarrassing to not even be functioning at a fourth-grade level. So that night, while my son was sleeping, I rifled through his backpack, pulled out his math textbook, and read the chapter on geometric forms. (Yeah, some parents read their kids' diaries and journals; I read their textbooks. You got a problem with that?)

The next afternoon at homework time, I slyly said to my son, "So, how 'bout them trapezoids?"

He looked at me blankly. "Huh?"

"Do you want me to go over quadrangles with you?" I asked him.

"No."

"Why not?"

"'Cause we're done with that. Now we're starting fractions."

Let's Just Agree to Disagree

It never ceases to amaze me how my husband's DNA and mine could combine to create two such totally different children. They are yin and yang, the sun and the moon, summer and winter... well, you get the idea.

She likes chocolate ice cream. He likes vanilla. She's a Coca-Cola girl. He drinks Sprite. He loves peanut butter and jelly. She'd rather eat dirt than peanut butter. He's up at the crack of dawn. She could sleep through a marching parade. He gels his hair. She runs screaming from the hairbrush. In his room, everything has a place. In her room, everything has a place on the floor. It's enough to drive a mother mad.

And because of their differences, or maybe just because they both breathe the same air, they fight with each other about everything.

"*Mom*, she hit me."

"Well, he closed the door on my hair."

"Well, she wouldn't get out of my room."

"Well, I had to go in his room because he took my Silly Putty."

"Well, I had to take her Silly Putty because she wouldn't turn her music down."

"Well, I had to turn it up because he was burping in my room."

"Why were you burping in her room?" I asked, taking the bait.

"To annoy her," he said and smiled. If nothing else, at least they're honest.

Eventually we worked it out. But most of the time I feel like a referee at a hockey game.

"Do you see Dad and I scream at each other when we argue?" I asked them.

"Yes," they said in unison.

"No, that's not screaming. That's disagreeing loudly," I explained. I should mention that one of the reasons we moved to the suburbs was for all the alleged quiet out here. After years of city living with the sounds of cars alarms, people yelling, and sirens going through my living room, my nerves were frayed. So we came out here... and got the sounds of car alarms, kids yelling, and lawn mowers blaring though our living room. Not much I could do about the cars and lawn mowers; but I decided, differences or no, my kids were going to stop yelling at each other and get along.

(I also decided at some point that I was not going to get any older than 35, which just goes to show you what kind of dream world I'm living in.)

Anyway, one day after another screaming match about whose turn it was to have control of the remote, I swooped in, grabbed it, and turned off the TV.

"This fighting has to stop," I said with parental authority. "From now on, every time I hear you guys fighting, you're both going to lose half an hour of TV time."

They looked panicked. I had known they would. Finally, I thought, a viable solution to the chaos.

Then my son whispered something in my daughter's ear and they both smiled.

"We're not fighting, Mom. We're disagreeing loudly."

Torturing me. That, they agree on.

Interlude II:
The Mother of All Reality Shows

Generic good-looking host: "Welcome back to *Survivor II: The Mother Lode*. It's year eight of the challenge and we have one contestant remaining: Tracy Beckerman. This week, our champion faces the ultimate challenge: As she recovers from extensive and painful gum surgery, we are sending her husband out of town on business for a week. But that's not all. Just to make things interesting, her daughter will come down with a nasty virus, the dog will get an ear infection, and the electricity in her kitchen will short out. Can she handle it all? Don't forget, the winner actually *gets* to go live on a desert island by herself for a full month!"

Host: "So, Tracy, are you ready for this?"

Beckerman: "Oh, sure. After the last challenge of finding fifty escaped crickets in my house, I'm ready for anything."

Host: "Don't forget, you can complain to your friends as much as you want, but you lose points if you whine to your husband. And if at any point you have to call in your mother-in-law for help, you will forfeit all winnings, and you will be voted out of the beach house."

Beckerman: "Got it."

[Fade out.]

Host: "Okay, let's skip ahead 24 hours. The champion

started out strong, but after a night of her daughter throwing up every hour, Beckerman is looking a little weary. She woke up to discover that none of the appliances in the kitchen were working and she has been unable to find an available electrician. She's holding it together even though she never got to take a shower today. But she doesn't know that we've arranged for her husband to call right about now."

[Phone rings.]

Beckerman: "Hello?"

Husband (over phone): "Hey, honey. How's it going?"

Beckerman: "Oh, you know… the usual. How about you?"

Husband: "Oh man, I'm exhausted. I had back-to-back meetings all day. I'm going back to the hotel, ordering up room service, and going to sleep."

Beckerman (covering the phone over with her hand): "AAAUUUGGGHHHHH!"

Husband: "Everything okay?"

Beckerman: "Sure. I was just thinking how nice it must be for you, when you're away from home and working so hard, not to have to worry about cleaning up after yourself or cooking any meals, and being able to go to sleep when you want without risk of being woken in the middle of the night by child, dog, or escaped cricket. Not that I'm complaining or anything. Because everything here is just peachy and you deserve all of that."

Husband: "Are you sure you're not complaining just a little bit?"

Beckerman: "No. Really. I'm good."

Husband: "Okay. Hey, you know what? The hotel has a spa. Maybe I'll go get a massage and sit in the jacuzzi before I get room service. That would help me unwind."

Beckerman: "A massage? A *massage???* I haven't even had a shower in two days!!! Our daughter has a temperature of 103, she threw up on her bed, on our bed, on me, basically everywhere except in the toilet; the dog has an ear infection; the power's out in the kitchen; my mouth is killing me; and I can't order up any [*bleep, bleep*] room service!"

Host: "Sorry, Tracy. You violated the No Whining to Your Husband rule. I'm afraid we're going to see you in the boardroom and someone is going to get fired."

Beckerman: "Yeah, well, I'm not too worried. As a mom, I don't get paid, I don't get benefits, and I don't get sick days or personal days. So technically, you can't really fire me."

Host: "Hmm. We're going to have to consult the judges about that and get back to you with a decision. In the meantime, tune in again as our champion faces her next challenge: *Another School Vacation.* Next time, on *Survivor II!*"

Rebel without a Minivan

A Spoonful of Cereal
Makes the Sugar Go Down

According to an unofficial study of these kinds of things, the typical American family has five boxes of breakfast cereal in their pantry.

We have 15.

I suppose this might make some sense if we had three times the average number of people in our household. But we don't. There are just four of us. And since I don't really eat the stuff, it means that the other people in my family are averaging five boxes of cereal each.

That, my friends, is a whole lot of bran.

The problem is everybody likes something different. My husband likes the kinds of cereal I call "Horse food." Basically it looks like hay to me. It's got lots of fiber and oat bran, and is so crunchy that I can hear him eating breakfast in the kitchen when I'm still in bed.

The kids, of course, like anything where sugar is the first ingredient and there is more nutritional value in the cardboard box than in the actual cereal. Their perfect breakfast food would be called "Super Sugar Frosted Cocoa Peanut Butter Choco-Puffs." However, since this may be the only one Kellogg's hasn't yet invented, we have to get five different cereals that the kids can mix together.

Lest you think I am a nutritional moron, I don't actually let the kids eat this junk for breakfast. The sugar cereal is a treat they can get after they eat some healthy cereal for breakfast. This is where the other five cereals come into play. Will they eat Dad's horse cereal? Neigh. So I have to get five other kinds of kid-friendly Cheerios clones for them to choose from.

Knowing this is the way of the world at my house, I try to hold the line at 15 because A) we have no more room in our pantry and B) people who have seen my pantry are starting to call me the Crazy Cereal Lady.

But one day, I made a critical error in judgement: I took the kids food shopping.

"Mom, come here quick," I heard my daughter yell from the next aisle. Imagining her buried beneath a toppled shelf of Campbell soup cans, I raced to her rescue.

But she was not buried under soup. She was not even in the soup aisle. She was, surprisingly, in the cereal aisle, where I found her completely intact and holding a box of New Super Frosted something or other.

"Look Mom, they have the new cereal I want to get. Can we get it? Can we get it? Can we get it? Huh? Huh? Huh? Can we????"

"No, we have enough cereal," I said firmly.

"But we don't! We're running low. And besides, this one has a third less sugar," she said pointing to the proclamation on the front of the box.

Ah, the "less-sugar" strategy. She had found my Achilles heel.

"Tell you what. I'll get it, but you have to finish one other box from the pantry before you can open this one."

"Deal," she said triumphantly.

The next morning we met in the kitchen.

"Mom, can I have breakfast?" she asked.

"Sure," I said opening the pantry door to expose the vast selection of cereal boxes. "What do you want?"

"Can you make pancakes?"

The Real Reason
People Get Road Rage

*M*onday, *November 28, 9:00 a.m.*

Dear Diary,

Today I have to renew my driver's license. I have a million things to do because the kids were home for four days over Thanksgiving and my house looks like a tornado struck Toys "R" Us. But I have to do it today because it expires tomorrow and I really don't want to have to run my errands on my son's scooter.

9:20 a.m.

The good news is there are no lines at this hour at the DMV. The bad news is they turned me away because I didn't have enough ID. They want something called "six points" of ID, and apparently my old driver's license and a copy of my birth certificate don't quite cut it. I have to assume I am not the only person who has made this critical error, and this is probably the reason why the DMV is empty.

P.S. All the DMV people seem really happy.

9:30 a.m.

I consulted the pamphlet they handed me and discovered I need one primary document valued at four points, such as my original birth certificate or a valid passport. Then I need two more points and something from the secondary document category, such as a debit card (one point) and a social security card (one point). The following are not considered acceptable forms of ID: my Neiman Marcus credit card, my Petco card, my National Honor Society card from high school, or my Bloomies Frequent Bra-Buyers Club card. I also need a document that proves my residence. I'm guessing the receipt from last night's pizza delivery doesn't count.

10:00 a.m.

I have to go to my safe deposit box to get my passport. But I can't find the darn key. I bet one of the kids took it to play "Prison Guard at Alcatraz." They put each other in the dog's crate and pretend to lock it. The prisoner has to try to escape, get off the island, swim through shark-infested waters, and make it to the TV room alive. The last time they played, my car key was missing for a week.

10:15 a.m.

I found the key. The children are safe from my wrath... for now.

10:25 a.m.

I got to my safe deposit box. No passport. Then I remembered I had used my passport to go to London this summer and never put it back in the box. I thought I recalled seeing it with my emergency roll of travel toilet paper.

10:45 a.m.

Home again. I've got my passport, but I forgot my social security card. I must have left it back in the safe deposit box. I think I may hurt someone.

11:00 a.m.

I got my social security card. The people at the bank think I'm a moron.

11:15 a.m.

Stopped at Dunkin' Donuts and got a big hunkin' cup of coffee because at this point, I'm ready to blow a gasket. I'm sure all the caffeine will calm me down.

11:40 a.m.

I am back at the DMV where no fewer than three people have examined my IDs. My guess is the first two people couldn't add up six points.

12:00 p.m.

Three hours later, I'm finally getting my new license. The DMV technician wants me to smile for the camera.

I wonder if they'll still renew my license if I tell her to bite me.

Peace on Earth AND
a Cherry Red Convertible

I think it's a shame that greed gets such a bad rap. I'm not even talking "seven deadly sin" kind of greed. Even simple, "how 'bout a little something for me" kind of thinking is frowned upon in our society. Why do we think that people are somehow more worthy of our esteem if they only wish things for others? What's wrong with wishing for something for ourselves?

Take the contestants in those beauty pageants. When asked what they wish for, they all say *world peace*. Do you believe them? I know I don't. I'm sure what they're really wishing is that Miss South Dakota would trip on the hem of her evening gown, Miss Kansas screw up her violin concerto, and Miss Hawaii get a big zit the night of the competition.

Then there's the month-long Christmas shopping feeding frenzy. In the midst of it, there were a bevy of retailers espousing "Peace on Earth, Good Will to All." Did they really want peace on Earth, or did they want their best fourth quarter profits ever? Unless Peace on Earth is a board game for sale, I know I don't believe them.

Of course I wish for world peace, too. But that's more of a hope-for kind of thing than an actual wish. On a more personal level, I'd be happy with simply having peace of mind, a peaceful evening without the kids squabbling, or a peace of pie without guilt (I know, wrong spelling; but homonyms count when you're wishing).

Wouldn't the world be a better place if we were honest about the fact that we all would like world peace *and* a piece of pie?

Kids are truthful. When I asked my kids what they wanted for Hanukkah, they directed me to the Amazon website to read their wish lists. They were each five pages long and world peace wasn't on either one.

We're not even supposed to be greedy on our birthdays. Yeah, you can ask for a sweater or a scarf, but just try asking for what you *really* want and watch the eyebrows rise. I've got a birthday coming up so I've been fielding just those questions. "I don't know," I say. "I don't really need anything." Which is true. But whoever said need and want are the same thing? I don't need a sports car, but I really want one. Sure it would be greedy and a mite presumptuous of me to hope that anyone would drop fifty grand on a sports car for me. But I can ask, can't I? It is, after all, what I wish for.

When I think about it, most of the things I want are beyond anyone's ability to give to me. I'd like someone to invent a way to stop traffic jams. I'd like someone to cure the common cold, and I'd like someone to find a way to get my dog to stop shedding. I'd like a house that cleans itself, laundry that washes itself, and kids who don't need baths. While we're at it, I'd like my body to have built-in sunscreen, eyelashes that don't need mascara, and thighs that repel cellulite.

Not too long ago, I wished for a terrific husband and wonderful children. I wanted a beautiful house and a big yard for the kids to play in. I wanted to live in a great town with good schools, nice neighbors, and a caring community. And I wished for the ability to stay home and raise my children and still have a rewarding part-time career.

Who says you can't get what you wish for?

That Little Itch Should Be
Telling Me Something

Once Labor Day had come and gone, I felt we were pretty much out of the woods as far as the scourges of summer go. As the days grew shorter, I realized that I was slapping fewer mosquitoes and pulling fewer weeds. One brisk morning, I even found myself donning a (gasp) sweatshirt. So imagine my surprise when I woke up one day with an itch. It started on my ankles. Then there were a few little bumps on my knees.

"Funny. The mosquitoes were really biting yesterday," I told my husband as I scratched my legs furiously.

"What mosquitoes?" he asked.

The next morning there were more bumps... on my wrists, neck, and hips. I showed them to a friend, who told me matter-of-factly that they looked like flea bites.

"I think we might have fleas in the house," I told my husband that night.

"We don't have a dog. Why would we have fleas?" he asked. Good point.

By day three, there were new bumps in some places, and the old bumps were starting to look a little, well, gnarly.

Finally I gave in and went to my dermatologist. She

gave my bumps a perfunctory glance and began writing on her prescription pad.

"It's flea bites, right?" I said.

"No," she said with an amused smile. "It's poison ivy."

I thought about the vine I had done battle with in my garden the week before Labor Day, and cursed myself for not noticing the telltale three-leafed calling card of this pesky plant.

I scratched in places I refuse to mention in mixed company and asked her what I should do.

"Get this cream," she said as she handed me a prescription. "And be prepared to itch like hell for up to six weeks."

I looked on my calendar and realized that six weeks would take me right up to Halloween. Who the heck has poison ivy on Halloween? Maybe I could dress up as a ghost with acne.

"Actually, you can get poison ivy any time during the year," my dermatologist informed me while I scratched. "The oils on the plant that cause the reaction are active all year long."

I thought about all the people in the world who truly deserved this torture: The guy who cut me off in the EZ-Pass lane and then realized he didn't have his EZ-Pass card. The trooper who ticketed me for doing 65 in a 55-mph zone while 18-wheelers passed me on the right doing 90. The guy who routinely lets his dog do its business on my lawn and then doesn't clean it up (yes, you — I know who you are!).

I got the cream, applied it liberally, and felt absolutely no relief whatsoever.

At this point, I not only itched rather badly, but I also started to resemble Linda Blair at her worst in *The Exorcist*. My mood pretty much matched hers, too.

"Take an oatmeal bath," suggested a friend. I did. It felt nice. Although some of the apples and cinnamon got in my hair. Ten minutes later, I itched again.

"Put toothpaste on the bumps," said another friend. I did. My bumps were minty fresh, but still itchy.

"Lie out in the sun to dry them up," said a third. I got a second-degree sunburn on top of my poison ivy. Finally, I called the wisest, most experienced person I know: my mother.

"Slather on Caladryl and then drink some scotch," she said.

"The Caladryl I understand," I told her. "But will the scotch really help?"

"It won't do a thing for the poison ivy," said my mother. "But after a drink, I guarantee you won't feel the itch anymore."

Exercising My Workout Options

After all my whining about life in suburbia, I finally realized what I'm missing by not living in the city. At my gym here, the only class they offer is spinning. At Gold's Gym in New York City, they have spinning, too. But they also offer belly dancing and strip aerobics (don't ask). At Crunch Fitness in New York, you can workout by doing cheerleading routines, or go to New York Health and Racquet for cardio hula. Would I take any of these classes if I lived in New York? Not on your life. After two kids, I certainly don't have the belly for belly dancing (not publicly, anyway), and I think my husband would shoot me if he found out I was doing strip aerobics. My daughter would die of embarrassment if she saw me practicing cheers and, most importantly, I just can't picture myself in either a cheerleading outfit or a grass skirt. But all that is beside the point. The point is that they're offered. Can you imagine belly dancing and strip aerobics in the 'burbs? Our local gyms are more likely to offer mall shopping as an aerobic activity than strip aerobics. Surely we, the women of suburbia, are more apt to get our heart rates up trying clothes on than taking them off.

Of course, I jest. Some of my best friends exercise, and

would no more consider shopping as a way to burn calories than doing laundry (although I might argue that ten loads up and down two flights of stairs does qualify as something of a workout).

I know there are people who like to exercise, but I'm not one of them. I find it as stimulating as, say, grocery shopping. It's one of those things I know I have to do, so I do it. Still, I can't help but think it might be a little more interesting if it were disguised as something like pole dancing or even a little salsa. For a couple of months I was into kickboxing, which was a nice break from the usual step-aerobics. But after awhile, throwing punches at myself in the mirror, even when I imagined my arch enemy's face in my reflection, just kind of lost its appeal. Perhaps it had something to do with the fact that I would run out of steam long before the instructor, who was eight months pregnant.

Still, I like the idea of exotic exercises to liven up my workout. But maybe classes like belly dancing aren't offered out here because they're simply too tame for us suburban moms. In New York, you get rid of your pent-up hostility by pushing people out of your way on the subway and screaming at taxi drivers. In the suburbs, we're expected to be more civilized, considerate, and polite. So what are we supposed to do with all that latent anger from waiting at the checkout for the cashier to get a key from the manager because she messed up somebody's purchase, and you're having a brain embolism because you have to pick up the kids from school in seven minutes?

I think out here in the suburbs, we need more aggressive workouts than they do in the city so we can vent our aggressions constructively. I would be the first to sign up for road-rage aerobics, which would simulate getting out of your car, jumping up and down in fury, and making obscene hand motions. That's a full-body workout I could relate to.

While I was pondering these exercise options, or lack thereof, my husband called and asked what I had done that day.

"Let's see. I went to the wholesale club and nearly got a hernia from lifting bulk packages of laundry detergent and dog food into my cart. I vacuumed dog hair off the floors in every room in the house, chased said dog for three blocks when he ran outside, and finally had to run home from school and back again because I locked my keys in the car."

"Wow," he exclaimed. "Sounds like you got a lot of exercise today."

Look at that. My life as a gym class. And I didn't even have to pay a monthly membership fee.

Add a "B" to Garage Sale and You Have Garbage

As a former city girl and apartment dweller, I always longed for the days when I would own a house with a basement and attic for storage.

However, as a homeowner, I soon learned that storage quickly turns into a trash receptacle for every unwanted gift, outgrown article of clothing, and, yes, impulse items purchased at other people's garage sales.

I have this philosophy: You don't ever actually find undiscovered treasures at garage sales. You find stuff that people bought at *other* garage sales with the intention to strip, paint, or repair but never do, and then it sits in your basement getting moldy until your husband threatens you with bodily harm if you don't get rid of it. This old stuff just rotates from one sale to the next until it eventually ends up in a heap on the corner for bulk pick-up.

So the truth is, if you go to five garage sales over the course of one summer, you'll probably see the same old stuff at one house on Labor Day weekend that you saw at another house Memorial Day weekend.

You've heard of the Circle of Life?

This is the Circle of Junk.

Still, like those before me and next door to me, I decided to join the ranks of the garage sale-challenged, optimistic that some neophyte bargain hunter might take my moldy bench off my hands so they have something to sell at their garage sale.

Now, I know there are a few intrepid shoppers who do actually turn a five-dollar dresser into a work of art. I am in awe of these people. I know a woman with eight kids whose rooms are filled with beautiful hand-painted armoires, charming little decoupaged chairs and tables, and stenciled dressers.

As I oohed and aahed over her furniture, I asked her where she got her stuff.

"Oh, I just picked them up at some garage sales and refinished them," she replied nonchalantly. I've tried this. However, I will often start on a project and then abandon it after the first sanding leaves me sweating and blistered. And I only have two kids.

The thing that truly amazes me about all this is knowing that the odds of finding something great at a garage sale are about the same as finding a husband who helps fold the laundry. Yet there are still those who will show up at a garage sale at 7:30 a.m., even though the signs say the sale starts at 9, so they can get first dibs on all the treasures.

My feeling is, if they want to show up at 7:30, they can help me dress and feed the kids, make the beds, and set up the tables for the sale, because I certainly won't be ready at 7:30. Then they can have first crack at my yogurt-maker if they want it.

I have friends who hold garage sales with alarming regularity, and they swear they make upwards of seven hundred dollars at every sale. At my last garage sale, my kids made more money selling lemonade and cookies than I made selling all my stuff combined.

That being the case, I thought perhaps I should consult the experts. "Put out brightly colored signs to attract people to your sale," the books say. "Make sure all the clothes are clean and pressed, the glasses and bric-a-brac are clean, and everything is grouped together by type and displayed on tables covered with attractive linens."

I say, if you pay two dollars for something that cost me twenty and I never used it, you can clean it yourself.

Of course my biggest obstacle to garage sale success is not the wrinkled linens I plan to sell, but the packrats in my family who refuse to give up the ghost on possessions way past their prime.

"You can't sell this toy," says my seven-year-old son. "I love this toy. It's my favorite!"

The toy in question is not the new Power Rangers Deluxe Transforming Megazord he pleaded for and got for his birthday two months ago, but the Little People Playhouse he got for his first birthday that hasn't seen the light of day since.

Similarly, as my husband carries the brimming boxes out to the garage, he spies his old eight-track cassette player and goes into cardiac arrest.

"You can't sell this," he exclaims. "Eight-tracks might come back in!"

Out from the box it comes and back into his closet it goes, alongside the transistor radio that only gets AM, the mirrored sunglasses circa 1980, and the *Miami Vice* wardrobe.

In his defense, I figure no one would pay money for an old eight-track player anyway.

Except perhaps another guy who's sure one day they'll come back in.

Interlude III:
In the Eye of the Mommy Storm

Joe Storm: "This is Inaccu-Weather meteorologist Joe Storm reporting from the beleaguered town of New Providence, New Jersey, where residents are bracing for another onslaught from Hurricane Tracy. This Category 4 hurricane is really unusual, returning to these parts at the same time every year and leaving a path of summer clothes sorted, packed away, and discarded in its wake. Joel Beckerman, an eyewitness to this bizarre yearly event, explains."

Beckerman: "We can usually feel the storm coming around Labor Day. By the time the kids start school, Hurricane Tracy's gone through all the closets and drawers and replaced all of the t-shirts and shorts with sweaters and long pants. It's a nightmare! It's still 75 degrees outside and we have nothing to wear!"

Joe Storm: "While Hurricane Tracy can be fearsome, it's the so-called 'calm after the storm' that really has the greatest impact. According to witnesses, the Beckerman children can be seen trudging down to the basement daily for weeks after the storm itself, searching through plastic storage bins for their summer clothes. Emily Beckerman explains."

Emily Beckerman: "It's dark and creepy down in the basement and I have to go down there all by myself to find my Barbie t-shirts. It's really hard on me. I'm only seven years old, you know!"

Joe Storm: "While similar hurricanes have periodically shown up in other homes across the country, this particular one seems to be the worst of the bunch. Fortunately, to date, there have been no casualties from this peculiar force of nature. A missing pet hamster was caught up in the storm one year, but it was later found in one of the plastic bins, unharmed.

"There is some good news on the storm front. Forecasters believe the hurricane may weaken slightly this year: A late summer beach vacation and early Jewish holidays have combined to slow the storm's usual progress. However, they caution that it will still be a formidable Category 3 storm when the eye hits land."

Joel Beckerman: "We've taken extra precautions this year. The kids have begun hoarding t-shirts under their beds and stashing bathing suits in their pillowcases. As long as Hurricane Tracy doesn't clean for dust bunnies between now and October, the kids' clothes should be safe."

Joe Storm: "That's some consolation for these storm-weary residents! In other weather-related news, a white tornado touched down in New Providence this weekend, removing mud, mildew, and grass stains from the Beckermans' lawn furniture, planters, and pool floats. Although brief in its duration, it left behind a pungent smell of ammonia that lingers on.

"More on that story later. Reporting from New Providence, I'm Joe Storm."

The Queen of Clean

Cleanliness Is Next
to Impossibleness

There are some things I do well and some things I
do fast. Unfortunately, I'm not always so good at doing both
at the same time. Take house cleaning, for example. When
I scrub the house, I am so thorough that I make Mr. Clean
look like an amateur. I leave no mattress unturned, no dust
bunny alive. However, I am so meticulous in my cleaning
that it can take me up to a week to clean the entire house
and so, by the time I'm done, I have to start all over again.
This doesn't leave much time for anything else, such as food
shopping, writing a column, or breathing. So several years
ago I came to the conclusion that although I may never
find anyone who can Tilex a bathroom like I do, and loathe
as I was to spend money on something I could do myself,
I knew I would have to hire someone else who could clean
well *and* fast, or my children would starve.

There are countless ads in the classifieds for cleaning
people, and numerous cleaning services advertised on the
sides of cars transporting their employees from one dirty
home to the next. However, for someone who has serious
dirt issues like I do, finding someone with the Mop and
Glo key to my heart could be a toughie.

I got really lucky with the last one: I appropriated her from my mother-in-law. Since I knew she was as particular about dust as I, I was pretty certain that the arrangement would work out. And it did... until my cleaning person left me a phone message that our relationship was over. It wasn't me, or the house, or even the threat of the lizard getting lost again that had done it. No, she was simply pregnant and, on doctor's orders, was in immediate house-cleaning retirement.

I was thrilled for her, because over the years we have become friends and I knew how much she'd wanted this. However, at the same time, I have to say I was a little freaked. Yes, I know, in the grand scheme of things, losing your housekeeper isn't as unsettling as, say, childbirth or divorce. But having been in this position once before, I knew it could be a challenge. So I immediately set out to raid the tills of my friends and family, only to find that they were reluctant to name names. Apparently a good cleaning person is as closely guarded a possession as a good babysitter.

I thought maybe I could fit in some Fantastic here, some Windex there, between the two zillion things on my to-do list. However, after almost two weeks, even my husband noticed that place was becoming a bit, er, unkempt.

"Hey, honey, did you notice that smell in the bathroom?" he asked one evening as I folded ten pounds of laundry.

"Yes," I said miserably.

"What is it?"

"It's a dirty bathroom! We need a new cleaning lady."

"Oh. Can you get right on that?" he asked as he wrinkled up his nose.

"*I've been on it,*" I shrieked hysterically. "*I can't find anyone!*"

He had the good sense to realize this was a touchy subject and quickly complimented me on how much laundry I'd gotten done that day. Only a man with a death wish would have suggested that I give up the quest and clean the house myself.

Still, I knew I had to do it. But daunted by the prospect of cleaning a pretty hairy and somewhat smelly house, which at this point would probably take me two weeks, I did what any sane woman would do: I went to Starbucks for a Venti Latte. As I pondered my choices, I suddenly noticed a teen-aged Starbucks employee vigorously sweeping the floors, and doing a darn good job of it, really, really quickly.

My heart beat faster. I thought I was in love.

"Hey," I yelled to him. "I have a cleaning offer for you. Good pay, less hours, and excellent benefits."

He laughed and kept sweeping.

"No, I'm serious," I said. "There are less coffee cake crumbs on my floor and the pay's probably better."

"You may be right," he responded. "But I bet the coffee's better here."

He had me there.

Add making coffee to the list of things I don't do well or fast.

Wash. Rinse. Scream. Repeat

On any given night in my house, I may have two kids in two bathtubs at one time. And while I'm busy washing one, the other may be taking the unsupervised opportunity to play "let's see how wet we can get the dog with the bathwater." They usually have a great deal of success with this since the dog is always a willing participant. And while they're at it, they do a commendable job of soaking the bathroom floor, the bathmat, and all the towels.

One night as I entered this waterlogged scene and shrieked, I freaked out the dog, who went tearing out of my daughter's bathroom, leaving a trail of bubbles and wet dog hair in his wake.

"Close the door so he doesn't soak the whole house," I shouted. Unfortunately, the only person who could help me was also soaking wet. Obedient child that she is, though, my daughter obligingly leaped out of the tub and slammed the bedroom door shut, missing the dog by a mile and spreading a fresh layer of water and bubbles on the floor.

Sighing in sodden resignation, I mopped up the floors and dried off the kids. I then had to track down the dog and give *him* a bath because he was half covered in Mr.

Bubble, which, if left to dry, would leave him looking like a doggy Don King.

While our dog likes to be splashed, he hates to be bathed, which typically means he and I will get equally wet as I desperately throw my arms around him to keep him from escaping his bathtub prison. Usually, if I'm lucky, only the bathroom and the dog and I get wet. But if the kids get wind of what I'm doing, they join in and get wet too (which usually means another rinse off for them as well). If the dog succeeds in his prison break, the whole house gets soaked, which is exactly what happened on this soggy night.

Eventually the kids, the dog, and the floors were dried, which left me with a mound of towels to wash. And then I was so sodden and covered in wet dog fur that I had to take a shower, too.

Finally, with everybody clean, combed, and pajamaed (well, not the dog), my husband walked in the door.

"Look how nice and clean everybody is, and the house and the dog, too," he said while he scooped the kids up in a bear hug and looked at me lovingly like I was Donna Reed. I, however, did not feel loving. I felt like I'd been on the *Titanic* and darn near drowned.

"The kids had a bath, the dog had a bath, the house had a bath," I said to him.

He nodded his head in understanding. Perhaps it was the mountain of wet towels piled at the top of the basement stairs. Or the dog hiding in his crate for fear I might come after him again with the bottle of Happy Puppy shampoo (there's a misnomer for you). Or maybe it was the smell of bubblegum bubble bath wafting through the house.

"You're off duty," he said. "Goodbye." And he whisked the kids upstairs for story time. I know I should have been appreciative. But instead all I could think was, "Oh sure, take over for story time. That's the easy part. But where were you half an hour ago when you needed a poncho, galoshes, and an ark to make it through this house dry?"

Muttering evil mommy things to myself, I made a cup of coffee, grabbed a magazine, and headed outside to sit on the deck and enjoy a few moments of quiet, dry, "me" time.

And then it rained.

My Toilet Runneth Over

My husband and I have this running joke: Whenever something in the house breaks, it always costs a thousand bucks to fix it. So I didn't bat an eye when the toilet had a nervous breakdown recently and the plumber came back with an estimate of a thousand dollars. My husband, however, almost had a stroke.

"A thousand bucks to fix the toilet!" he shrieked over the phone to me. "Are you nuts?"

"Well, actually, it's a thousand bucks to fix three toilets and two sinks," I explained.

Silence. "You lost me," he said.

I guess I could understand his confusion. Earlier that day I had called him in hysterics when my son flushed the toilet in the kids' bathroom, and it kept on flushing: pouring over the top of the toilet, onto the floor, through the floor, into the basement... well, you get the idea. Somewhere in the back of my Ms. Fix-it mind, I recalled learning that when something like this happens, you should *not* scream, grab the kids and the dog, and run for higher ground. Rather you should get on your knees in the middle of the mess and turn off the stupid water valve behind the toilet.

So I did. Then I mopped up the mess. And then I

called my husband on his business trip, because, naturally, he's always on a business trip when these things happen.

"He's in a meeting," said one of his *people*. "Is this an emergency?"

"No. Just tell him the toilet blew up and he should call me when he gets a chance." Thirty seconds later, my husband was on the phone.

"I turned off the valve," I told him. I was very proud of myself. "What should I do now?"

"Call-a-plumb-er," he said as though speaking to someone who didn't understand English. "And make sure you get an estimate before he does anything."

I spent an hour making calls and went through four plumbers before I found one who would A) answer the phone, B) agree to come the same day, and, C) not laugh in my face when I asked him to come the same day.

Finally a guy came — when he actually said he would — and even wore his pants around his waist where they belonged. First he went to the sick toilet.

"Do your kids put any strange things in here?" he asked.

"You mean like Barbie heads, Harry Potter potions, and dead crickets?" I asked.

"Yeah."

"Hardly ever," I told him.

Here's the part where we got to the $1000 estimate. After checking the toilet, he asked me if there were any other toilets or faucets that weren't working properly.

"I want to see if this is an isolated issue or if there's a problem with the central plumbing," he said. I had no idea what he was talking about, but after I turned on all the sinks and flushed all the toilets, he told me that the pipes were clear but the doohickeys in the other two toilets and the thingamajigs in two sinks all had to be replaced. (Okay, he didn't really call them that, but damned if I can remember their real names.)

Pricetag for all the doohickeys and thingamajigs: $1000.

I called my husband back.

"He's in another meeting," said one of his *people*. "Is this an emergency?"

"No. Just tell him I'm about to write a check for a thousand dollars and he should call me when he gets a chance." Thirty seconds later, my husband was on the phone.

"Are the other toilets and sinks working?"

"Yeah."

"Then just have him fix the one that's not and call another plumber for a second estimate on the stuff that's not an emergency," he said.

"Call another plumber???" I shrieked. *"Are you nuts?"*

I explained that this was the only plumber in the universe who had responded to my crisis and hadn't mooned me when he bent over to work on the pipes.

What I didn't say was that I didn't want to spend another hour on the phone or waiting at home between nine and one for a guy to show up to tell me my doohickeys and thingamajigs needed to be replaced. But my husband was adamant that we only fix the toilet that was broken.

"Okay," I said to him. I hung up, and went to look around for a few more Barbie heads.

Coming out of the Closet

$\mathbf{W}$hen I lived in the city, the change of seasons went something like this: I took my summer clothes from the front of my only closet and moved them to the back. Then I took my winter clothes from the back of the closet and moved them to the front.

Done. Finished. End of story.

There were no tires to change on the car because I didn't have one. Likewise, no lawn furniture to put away, no pool to cover, no flowerpots to empty, no screen doors to replace, no gutters to clean out, and no leaves to rake.

In fact, since there were no trees on my street, and therefore no leaves to turn color, my only indication that we were headed into fall came when the sidewalk vendors switched their wares from cheap sunglasses to cheap scarves.

I thought I had it pretty good compared to my friends in the 'burbs. That is, until winter set in. While they were cruising around in their toasty minivans, I was hoofing it to the subway through wind tunnels that made the frozen tundra look like Club Med.

So when I finally took the plunge and moved out of the city, I looked forward to the extra work involved in the change of seasons, secure in the knowledge that my post-autumnal existence would be a kinder and gentler one.

Our first winter the boiler died.

"Call the super to fix it," I told my husband stupidly.

"There *is* no super," he said. "We're homeowners now, honey. We have to get someone in, which could take a couple of days, and then pay them an obscene amount of money to look at the thing so they can tell us it's beyond repair, and then pay an even more obscene amount of money to buy a new one."

"Oh."

My kids thought it was pretty nifty that we could see our breath as we ate breakfast at the kitchen table, but I was not as amused.

The next winter, with a brand-spanking-new boiler, I was secure in the knowledge that we wouldn't have a repeat of the previous winter's catastrophe.

And then there was this itty, bitty winter storm that knocked the power out in town for two days, and on my block for a week. My kids thought it was pretty cool when we buried our food in the snow so it wouldn't go bad, but I didn't share their enthusiasm for that, either.

Which brings us to winter number three in suburbia, and I wasn't quite as secure in my warmth potential as I had been. The day we were scheduled to close the pool, I begged my husband to leave it open just a little while longer.

"Honey," he said as we stood shivering next to the pool filter. "Halloween is in two weeks. It's 58 degrees out. Even the ducks aren't swimming anymore. I really think it's time."

"One more week," I pleaded. He shook his head in resignation and went back inside.

Just to show him I was ready to face reality, I went down to the basement, hauled the crates of winter clothes up two flights to the bedrooms, loaded the crates back up with summer clothes, and lugged them back downstairs.

With my children's closets and mine brimming with new, un-magic-marker-stained sweatshirts, sweaters, and corduroys, I studied my work with satisfaction and gave in to the inevitable.

And then the next day, it turned warm. Downright balmy, in fact.

"Good thing we didn't close the pool yet," said my husband. "Let's all go for a swim. Where are the kids' bathing suits?" he asked, rummaging through their drawers.

"I packed them away," I said sullenly.

"Why did you pack them away?" he asked.

"Because you said it was time. You said even the ducks weren't swimming. You said, you said!!!"

"Well, I was wrong."

"Excuse me? What was that?" I cupped my ear. "Did you say you were *wrong?*" I love that word. But only when other people say it.

Happily, I dragged the clothing crates back upstairs, pulled out the bathing suits and towels, and we all enjoyed a lovely day of fun in the sun.

The next morning, as I picked out shorts and t-shirts for my kids to wear, my husband appeared in the doorway in a sweater and long pants.

"Better pick out some warm clothes for them," he said nonchalantly. "They say it's gonna be really cold today."

Without missing a beat, I went to their closets and pulled some winter clothes from the back and put their summer clothes away in the front.

Done. Finished. End of story... until spring, of course.

The Fungus among Us

I never thought I'd be one of those suburban moms who talks about cleaning problems, but I have to admit it: I have fungus issues.

In the past I think I've handled those pesky minor battles with mildewed tile grout, scummy shower curtain liners, and other assorted moldy nuisances with appropriate reactions. Tilex in hand, I spray like a maniac, and moments later, I am fungus-free. But one day, I happened to lift up the rubber bath mat in the kids' bathroom to rinse the tub after one of them took a particularly filthy bath, and saw black. Literally.

The bottom of this formerly white bath mat was covered in a living, breathing black mold that pretty much completely grossed me out.

I don't gross out easily. I routinely have to clean up after numerous pets, not to mention two kids and a husband, so being grossed out is something I've gotten used to. But this bath mat was beyond gross. It was the bath mat from the black lagoon. An entire civilization of stinky fungus breeding in my bathtub. Mutant mold from outer space. I was sure if I didn't get rid of it immediately, it would continue to multiply and grow until it enveloped my entire bathroom, then my house, and eventually the world. Yes, it was my duty as a member of the human race to kill it.

At this point in the story, you're probably wondering how, as a world-class homemaker, I managed to miss the underside of my kids' bath mat.

I hadn't. The cleaning ladies had. I had assumed they were routinely scouring under the bath mat and then returning it to its original location. But I guess we'd never discussed the bath mats when I'd hired them two years prior and given them a list of things to clean. Floors? Yes. Windows? Yes. Bath mats? Apparently not.

Okay, so I'm an idiot. And an idiot with a disgusting bath mat to boot. But rather than dwell on unconstructive negative self-blame, I decided to harness that self-disgust into some positive mold-ridding energy.

First I broke out the Tilex.

(Note to self: Write letter to Tilex people to inform them that product doesn't work on Mutant Mold from Outer Space).

Then I tried some scouring powder. But still some of the mold survived the attack.

(Note to self: Soft Scrub with Bleach stains expensive clothing).

Then I whined.

"I can't get rid of the mold on the bath mat," I cried to my husband one day. He gave me a blank stare.

"So spend, like, seventy-nine cents and buy a new one," he shrugged.

"No, I like this one. And it's not about the money,

anyway," I protested. "I have to save this bath mat... and the world."

Another blank stare. I had forgotten: the mold might be from outer space, but men are from Mars, and there was no way my husband was going to process the magnitude of my crisis unless it involved a trip to the hardware store.

In desperation, I dumped the bath mat into the washing machine with detergent, bleach, and any other cleaning products I had in the laundry room that looked toxic. Then I turned on the hot water and waited.

Half an hour later I took out the bath mat and the mold was gone. So was most of the bath mat. Pristine white and riddled with holes: It was now a bath net.

I appeared before my husband, sweaty and disheveled from my ordeal, clothes stained with scouring powder residue, holding the remains of my former bath mat.

"I've got good news and bad news," I told him. "The good news is I got the mold off the bath mat."

"Hallelujah!!" he exclaimed in mock excitement.

"The bad news is I killed the bath mat. But at least I saved us from the mutant mold," I said.

He eyed me fearfully. "Great. But who's going to save us from you?"

The Not-So-Perfect Mother

Waiting in the schoolyard for my son to be dismissed, I overheard two moms talking about housecleaning. "There's a fabulous new product out," one told the other. "Some kind of cleaning wipes for your bathroom. They're already pre-soaked with cleaning fluid, so you can just pop one out any time and presto, a fresh, clean bathroom!"

Ha! *My* house, on a fairly good day, looks like a nuclear bomb went off in the middle of Chuck E. Cheese.

Then there's the laundry. I have two laundry baskets and I leave them both in the basement. One is filled with clean clothes, the other dirty. I don't have time to fold, so when someone needs something clean, they strip in the basement, toss the dirties in one basket, and fish something clean from the other. My family may not be pressed and creased in all the right places, but they do have clean underwear.

And did I mention dinner? My specialty is anything with the word AND in the middle: macaroni *and* cheese, spaghetti *and* meatballs, hamburger *and* helper (okay, that's not the real name, but it is essentially an *and* meal). And let me tell you, baby, when it comes to heating and reheating, Wolfgang Puck could learn a thing or two from me.

Gourmet, you gather, I am not. Not that my family is

complaining. Given the choice between The Four Seasons and McDonald's, a Happy Meal would win out every time.

What's my point? Well, I'm not Carol Brady. I don't think I'm even half as domestic as Carmella Soprano. But when I quit my full-time job to stay home and take care of my kids, I had visions of a beautifully kept home, sumptuous meals, and happy, well-adjusted kids who thrived on my constant attention.

What Disney movie did I think I was starring in?

I have a friend; I'll call her Wonder Woman. Wonder Woman has the beds made, the dishes done, is showered and dressed and has her three kids dressed before Regis even introduces his first guest. She could change a diaper, sew a button, and floss her teeth all at the same time. She is president of her P.T.A. and led the fundraising drive to build a new playground in her town while she was pregnant, then helped *build* the darn playground two weeks after she gave birth. Wonder Woman makes all her kids' Halloween costumes and even one for herself, just for handing out her home-baked M&M peanut-butter chocolate-chip nuggets.

"How do you do all that and still play with the kids?" I ask in amazement.

"Who has time to play?" she says.

Then there's my other friend, Fashion Mom. She also quit her job to stay home with her kids. Then she hired a full-time, live-in nanny who stays home with the kids while Fashion Mom goes shopping at the mall. I don't envy her… but she does have really nice clothes.

My husband says it's not important to him to have

a clean house or clean underwear. He could buy new underwear if he ran out. He also doesn't care if I'm wearing brown clothes when everybody *knows* the color this season is gray. The important thing is that I use all my creative talents and loving, nurturing skills to make my children's daily existence a meaningful one.

I imagine this doesn't mean exercising my unqualified skill at pushing the play button on the VCR so they can watch *Toy Story* for the millionth time while I use my pop-up, presoaked bathroom-cleaner wipes to freshen my bathroom.

I do know that my most important job is to spend time with my children, not my washing machine or my vacuum cleaner or my credit card. Still, it's tough to remember that when Wonder Woman tells me she has all three kids bathed and fed before their father walks in the door, or when Fashion Mom shows up at my house in her *gray* designer frock without a trace of SpaghettiOs anywhere on her.

That's when I call *my* mother.

"Tell me something," I say. "I remember when I was little, you used to get down on the floor and play dolls with me, and we would cook together, and you would let me put on your makeup when you were getting dressed to go out. But I don't remember if the house was clean or what you wore or what you made for dinner."

"Isn't that the point?" my mother responds.

Smart lady.

Interlude IV:
To Grandmother's House We Go

"Hey, Mom, are we at Grammy's yet?"

"No, we just left the house."

"Well, how much longer is it?"

"Five minutes less than the last time you asked me."

"I'm bored."

"Do you want to play the license plate game?"

"No. That's boring. How much longer?"

(Sigh.) "About forty-five minutes."

"Forty-five minutes?!?!? That's like a year. I'm gonna be old by the time we get there."

"No, *I'm* going to be old by the time we get there."

"I'm hungry. No, I mean thirsty. No, yeah, thirsty."

"Drink your water."

"I finished it."

"The whole bottle?"

"Yeah. Oh! I have to go to the bathroom."

"Of course you do, because you just drank a whole bottle of water. Can you wait?"

"No, I have to go right now. It's an emergency!!! I have to go! I have to go!"

"Okay, hold on while we find a place to stop."

"Can I get something to eat when we stop?"

"No, you just had breakfast."

"But I'm so hungry I might die of hunger!!!"

"I thought you were thirsty."

"I'm hungry *and* thirsty, and I have to go the bath-room, really, really bad!"

"Hang on. The exit is coming up."

"Can I get a doughnut?"

"*No!* We'll eat when we get to Grammy's."

"But that's not for a whole 45 minutes."

"Actually, it'll be longer."

"Why?"

"Because we have to stop so you can go to the bathroom."

"Never mind. I can hold it in. Mom, Josh is annoying me."

"She annoyed me first."

"No, he did. He leaned on my side."

"Both of you cut it out."

"I wish I never had a brother. I'm not talking to you for the rest of the trip."

"Fine with me."

"Hey, Josh, do you want to play I Spy?"

"No. I'm playing my Game Boy."

"Game Boy is stupid."

"No, you're stupid."

"*Mommmm!*"

"Hey, who wants to watch a DVD?"

"I do."

"I do."

"Put on *Finding Nemo!*"

"Can we watch the whole thing?"

"No. Only about half."

"Awwww. I wish we were in the car longer."

The Road Less
Traveled with Children

Greetings from Disney World

Walt Disney was mistaken. It is *not* a small world after all. If the line to get into Space Mountain is any indication, it is a big, *big* world. And everyone who lives in it is waiting to get on this ride.

Yes, we are in the happiest place on Earth. That is, if your idea of a good time is to stand in line with hundreds of kids melting down from hunger, exhaustion, and overstimulation.

We purposely chose this week to go to Disney World to avoid the notorious lines. We were told that this was the best week to go because ours is the only state that has our schools closed for teachers' conferences. If that's the case, however, then I think the whole state of New Jersey had the same idea as we did.

I should have known I was in trouble when my sister-in-law, a respected Disney veteran and our travel companion, told me we had to reserve tickets for a character breakfast three months, two hours, and thirty minutes to the day before the breakfast we wanted.

And when I called three months, two hours, and forty-five minutes ahead of the date, they were already completely booked.

Then the happy folks at Disney called me a month before our trip to tell us they had canceled our Disney hotel reservation.

"We're sorry. We decided to close that resort for renovations the week you're planning to be here."

"But I made those reservations last January," I protested.

"It's not a problem," she said cheerfully. "We can put you up at another moderate resort instead."

"Oh no. If you cancel my reservation, you can put me up a deluxe resort!" I must have been on speakerphone. I heard laughing in the background.

"Here's anther moderate resort that's nice," she said, naming my last-choice hotel. "I'm sure you and your husband and two kids will be very comfortable in our cramped 10x10-foot rooms with two double beds and a trundle. You should be grateful we're not booking you in the trailer park next to the petting zoo because you paid for this trip with frequent flier miles, which basically means no money for us."

Okay, she didn't say that. But that's what she meant.

I figured we'd only be in the rooms to sleep, so what was the difference. So we went. And by day three, I was convinced that if one more person wished me a magical day, I was going to blow.

"Sorry. The Peter Pan ride is closed for repairs. But have a magical day!"

"Sorry. Your daughter's not tall enough for this ride she's been waiting to go on for three days. But have a magical day!"

"Sorry. You have a regular park-hopper pass and you

need an ultimate park-hopper pass to get into this attraction, otherwise it's $40 per person. But have a magical day!"

The only thing magical was the fact that I hadn't punched anybody yet.

I finally decided that I needed an attitude adjustment if I was going to make it through two more theme parks, another character dinner, and the Hoop-Dee-Doo Revue (don't ask).

So I did what any sane mother would do. I bought Mickey Mouse ears, ate Mickey Mouse pancakes, and told my kids if they didn't stop whining and start having a good time, next year we would spend our vacation at the mall.

"No! Not the *mall!!!!*"

Thus, the whining ceased (temporarily of course) and we all started to have a good time. By the end of each day, my children, covered in goo from the countless ice pops, gummy things, and fried who-knows-whats we fed them as we waited in line, fell asleep on the bus, dreaming of Buzz and Woody, beauties and beasts, and seven assorted dwarfs.

Five days later, on the plane back home, I said to the kids, "So, do you miss Disney?"

"Nah. It was fun, but it's good to go home."

Good? I'd say downright magical.

What I Did on
My Winter Vacation

When I learned that the islands of Turks and Caicos in the Caribbean average 350 days of sunshine a year, I felt pretty confident that it would be a good place to spend our winter break. What were the odds that one-fifth of the yearly rain would fall while we were on vacation there?

Yeah, well, I don't usually win at horse races, either.

The good news was, for the first three days of our vacation, I didn't have to worry about any of us getting sunburn. The bad news was, when you go to a place for fun in the sun, there ain't no fun if there ain't no sun.

At least there was a game room the size of a gymnasium for just such an emergency. My son spent the better part of those three days becoming the master of the Sega universe. My daughter, on the other hand, spent her time becoming the whining queen of the Caribbean.

"Do you want to see what's happening in the kids' club, Em?"

"No, the kids' club is boring."

"Do you want to go to the game room?"

"No, the game room is boring."

"How about limbo, or reggae lessons or foosball?"

"Boring, boring, and more boring." Apparently we had spent the equivalent of one month's salary so my son could play video games and my daughter could be bored. We could do that for free at home.

Nine meals and a dozen downpours later, we began to get on each other's nerves.

"You're a dummy."

"Well, you're a double-dummy."

And that was just my husband and me.

When the kids started to annoy each other incessantly, we finally got fed up.

"Can't you find one nice thing to say about your sister?" my husband asked my son.

He thought for a minute. "She's got nice nostrils."

She does, actually.

Personally, I didn't see anything wrong with this vacation. I didn't have to cook or clean or make the beds or do laundry. There was no dog to feed. Ditto the lizard. I didn't have to be the homework czar or carpool queen or dry-cleaning delivery person. Except for the matter of the whining children, as far as I was concerned, this vacation was a slam dunk.

Of course, I thought, a tan would definitely put it over the top. But the forecast was for scattered showers all week (better, I suppose, than the monsoon-like conditions we'd had so far). So I prayed to the sun gods and asked that they show a little kindness to us, because, after all, it was my birthday on Christmas and that should count for something.

And lo and behold, the next day, the sun shone. Meekly

at first, and then progressively better with each passing hour.

"Yippee!" I crowed as we slathered lotion on the kids. "Let's hit the beach."

So we sunned. We surfed. We snorkeled. We sailed. And then we ate lunch. We bonded as a family over conch salad and grilled grouper.

And then my son said, "After lunch can I go to the game room?"

"What, are you nuts?" I sputtered. "The sun finally came out. Don't you want to be on the beach?"

"The beach is boring," announced the whining queen of the Caribbean.

I Have a Lipstick in My Pocket
and I'm Not Afraid to Use It

There are some rules I understand, and some I completely don't get. For example, it makes a lot of sense that they don't allow cameras when you take a tour of the White House. Here you are at the home of the president, the epicenter of our government, the place where critical political decisions are made every day... and they don't want you taking pictures. *That* makes sense to me. Similarly, you are not allowed to bring firearms (okay), sharp, pointy objects (sure), lighters (ditto), and of course, makeup.

Makeup?

At what point did mascara and lipstick become a threat to our national security? Personally, I find that I'm more threatening without makeup, but clearly the White House administration disagrees.

We had to go through quite a bit of security clearance to tour the White House. I had to write our congressman two months in advance, give our social security numbers, dates of birth, and the name of the first pet I had as a child. Then I had to remember to bring our letter of confirmation and all of our passports as proof of our IDs. I made it through the whole process and was granted permission to pass through the White House gates — until they found my lip gloss.

Secret Service Guy: "I'm sorry, ma'am, you can't go in with that lipstick."

Me: "It's lip balm."

SSG: "That item is not allowed on the tour."

Me: "But my lips are chapped, and besides, it's cherry-flavored."

SSG: "It's you or the lipstick, ma'am."

Me: "Fine! But I'm writing my congressman and I'm CC-ing the Chapstick people, too."

Ultimately I surrendered the lip balm, but I had the Secretary of Makeup note that I did so under duress and, I believe, in violation of my constitutional rights.

"Isn't there a clause about our right to life, liberty, and the pursuit of unchapped lips?" I asked my husband. He shook his head.

"I think I also remember an amendment about the right to bear lip balm," I added. He rolled his eyes. I made a mental note to return to the National Archives later and check the original documents — assuming, of course, that I made it through those metal detectors with my deadly tube of clump-free mascara.

Meanwhile, back at the White House, I tried to figure out what the issue was with the makeup thing because as far as I can remember, no one has ever overthrown a government with a compact and a blush brush. Maybe they were worried that someone would use their lipstick to color in Martha Washington's lips on her portrait in the

East Room. This would be a fairly easy thing to do if not for the stanchions and ropes that keep you fifty feet back from the artwork, or the two armed security guards positioned directly behind the ropes, or the security cameras in every corner, or the sharpshooters behind every window.

Yeah, I could see how this would be a concern.

I finally gave up trying to discern the random policies of an otherwise level-headed and clear-thinking administration and tried to enjoy the tour.

As we were leaving, my husband turned to me and said, "That tour guide really knew some great stuff about the White House, didn't he?"

"Really?" I said. "I must have missed it. I was too distracted."

"By what?" he asked.

"He had really chapped lips."

Getting a Kick out of
Flying with Children

I'm not one to judge people by their appearances, but when I saw the guy who was seated in front of my daughter on the plane ride home from our vacation, I just knew he wasn't a "child person." My first clue was the way he started rolling his eyes when he saw my kids enter the row behind him. There was the way that he started glaring at me through the crack in the seats while we were still sitting on the runway. And then there was the thinly veiled contempt as he asked me to have my daughter stop kicking his seat.

"Oh, sure. I'm sorry. No problem," I said, truly apologetic. "Don't kick the seat," I told my daughter. Five minutes later, I got the glare again.

"She's still kicking," said the guy.

"I'm sorry, but her legs stick straight out into the back of your seat," I said back through the crack between the seats. I turned to my daughter again. "Please try not to kick the man's seat."

"I'm not," she said defiantly. As we took off, he gave me another glare. "I can't get comfortable," he growled a few minutes later. "This *has* to stop."

I was not insensitive to what this guy was going through. I've been there. I've done my share of grimacing at the young children and crying babies surrounding my seat on long plane rides in the past. But I've also recognized and had some compassion for parents who tried really, really hard to keep their children as reigned in and unobtrusive to the other passengers as possible.

Clearly, he was not as understanding.

"So what are you going to do about it?" he demanded. I looked at how he had his seat reclined *all* the way back in my daughter's lap, and realized that she didn't have room to put her feet anywhere else. I was about to point this out to him. Instead I said, "She's a little girl. She's doing her best."

"That's not good enough," said Mean Plane Guy.

My husband, sitting across the row from me, finally got wind of the problem and stood up to throw some more testosterone into the mix.

"Is there a problem here?" he asked innocently.

"Yeah, this self-centered jerk put his seat in our daughter's lap and is having a hissy-fit because her feet keep brushing the back of it." Okay, I didn't say that. But only because I didn't know how big the Mean Plane Guy was and I didn't want my husband to get beat up.

"She keeps kicking my seat," whined MPG to my husband.

"Change seats with her," my husband said to me.

"But Daddy," cried my daughter, "I want the window!"

"I can't sit here for five hours with her kicking my seat," chimed in MPG. I considered offering him a parachute and directions to the emergency exit, but thought better of it.

"Enough!" bellowed my usually soft-spoken husband. "Would you please just switch with her," he said to me. I looked at the woman sitting in front of me, who had been monitoring this whole exchange somewhat uncomfortably. She nodded that it was okay if my foot-happy daughter moved in behind her. So we switched.

Mean Plane Guy then smiled, donned his headset, and reclined his seat back into my lap. I put down my tray table and laid out some cards so the kids could play a game. Then I crossed my legs, and kicked the guy's seat.

Skiing and Careening Downhill
Are Not the Same Thing

My husband comes from a family of skiers and has skied since he was six years old. When I was growing up, the only time we went out into the snow was to shovel the driveway. Ever since the birth of our children, it's been my husband's dream that we, too, would be a family of skiers. It has been *my* dream to sit by the fire in the ski lodge and sip hot chocolate while they ski.

This is what they call a conflict of interest.

It's common knowledge that children are better at learning new skills than adults. This is why there are toddlers who can speak three languages and adults who can barely speak one. This is also why my two children, at ages six and eight, have already mastered downhill skiing, while I, who have been skiing the same length of time as they, have only mastered downhill falling.

However, I didn't want to be a wet blanket, so I agreed to at least try. We booked a family ski vacation to Vermont. We arrived late at night, woke early the next morning, and with our car loaded with skis, boots, poles, outerwear, underwear, and whatnot, we pulled out of the driveway of our condo rental.

"Which way to the mountain?" asked my husband, Joe Skier.

I looked at my map and said confidentially, "Left." For fifteen minutes we went one way while all the other cars passed us in the opposite direction. Still we drove on.

"How much further?" asked Joe Skier.

"I don't know. The rental agent said we were literally one minute from the mountain," I said, my confidence waning. We pulled off to the side and for the first time looked back in the other direction. There was the mountain looming as big as, well, a mountain, with all the trails and lifts in full view. Had we actually looked up as we pulled out of the driveway, it would have been pretty hard to miss the ski resort directly behind our condo.

"Where are the ski slopes? I can't find the ski slopes. There's this big mountain in the way," yelled my first-born (clearly his father's son).

"How could you not see that?" asked Joe Skier.

"How could you not look in your rearview mirror?" I retorted. He harrumphed. I pffed. The kids snickered and we turned the car around. I could see where this vacation was going.

Now, this was not my first time skiing. We'd had a couple of weekend outings before, so I knew enough to skip the bunny slopes and start with the slopes for those who could ride the chairlift without falling off. But conquering the chairlift is one thing; learning how to avoid careening into the woods when you're moving faster than five miles per hour is quite another. I decided to join a group class of eleven other uncoordinated adults in the hope that I could learn enough to keep up with my kids, or, at the very least, avoid ending up in a full body cast.

I gave our instructor the benefit of the doubt, listened to his directions, and somehow made it to the bottom of the first slope without eating snow. However, when our group reassembled and I asked him where one of our classmates was, the instructor turned, looked around, and shrugged. "I guess we lost him," he said, nonplussed. Suddenly the first aid team flew past us, alarms blaring and rescue sled in tow. I decided if I wanted to live to obsess about bathing suit season, I needed to book a private lesson.

The next day I met my new ski instructor from Australia. "Okay, mate. Let's go to the top of this hill and work on your parallel turns," he said.

"That's not a hill," I shrieked, looking up the mountain. "That's a cliff!" But I followed him, believing that if this guy could scuba dive in Australia without being eaten by a great white shark, he could get me to the bottom of the Easy Rider slope with all my appendages intact.

And so we skied. We turned. In one hour, I made more progress than in all my other ski outings combined.

Finally I reconvened with my husband and boasted proudly, "Watch me, watch me, I learned everything! I can ski. I can do parallel turns!" I pushed off with my poles, made two beautiful turns, and then wiped out.

"That was great, honey! Get up and do it again," he encouraged.

Get up?

Tales of an Intrepid Traveler

I had a hunch, an inkling, call it a premonition of sorts, that our trip to Italy might somehow end up becoming... how do you say it in Italian? A *nightmarissimo*. I think it was those two little words, "connecting flight," that led me to believe there might be trouble. So on a whim, I packed an extra outfit and some toiletries in a carry-on bag.

"Aren't you being just a little bit paranoid?" my husband asked as I shoved one more pair of underwear into the bulging carry-on.

"We have a connecting flight," I told him as I sat on the bag to zipper it. "Connecting flight means you get on another plane, but your suitcase doesn't."

"That's not going to happen," he said with the smug assurance of people who only fly domestically.

"No, really," said I.

"No way," said he. But when we finally got to Florence...

"No suitcase," said the airline representative.

We waited on line behind an alarming number of people in the same situation and left a detailed description of our missing belongings with someone who clearly could not have cared less.

And then we waited.

And waited.

And waited some more.

Not that we just sat around. We merrily explored Tuscany in our two outfits each, and returned to our hotel each day expecting a suitcase, which did, in fact, finally come — the day before we were due to fly home. I say "due to fly home," because we didn't actually fly home the day we were due. This time they didn't lose our suitcase. They lost the whole plane.

We learned this when we got to Florence to catch our flight to Rome, and waited for them to call the flight. We waited some more (we were getting good at this). Finally someone showed up, shrugged her shoulders, and said, "Sorry, the flight has been canceled." And then she left.

I've had doctor appointments canceled. My babysitter has canceled. I even had a C-section canceled. But I've never heard of an airline just up and cancel a flight an hour before takeoff, for no clear reason.

We were, how do you say it in Italian, *multo hystericalo.*

Intrepid travelers that we had now become, we raced out of the terminal, got back in the rental car we had just returned, and drove like Ferrari owners three hours down to Rome to try to catch our flight.

We missed it by ten minutes.

Had this been someone else's travel story, at this point I might have laughed. But my husband and I were not so amused. Even less so when we found out there were no other flights to New York that day. And no room on the flights the next. Eventually I had a nervous breakdown in front of the right people and we got seats on a flight home.

Tears came to our eyes when we saw our suitcase tumble off the baggage claim carousel.

As we went through customs, the agent opened our passports and said, "Welcome home. Do you have anything to declare?"

"Yes," I said. "I am *never* flying on that airline again!"

Interlude V:
The 2003 Suburban
Summer Olympics

"It's another beautiful day here at the Suburban Summer Olympics, where we're entering our tenth day of competition. What do we have to look forward to today, Allison?"

"Well, Bob, our leading competitor, Tracy Beckerman, is starting to show some signs of exhaustion as we look at another day of record-breaking temperatures. Beckerman is nearing the end of the Getting the Kids off to Camp marathon. She just finished the Applying the Sunscreen to the Struggling Kids part of the competition and is preparing for the Mounting of the Backpacks and Ushering the Kids onto the Camp Bus segment. They're heading down the driveway and — oh no, one of the kids has decided she wants to change shirts! That's going to cost Beckerman some time."

"Too bad!"

"Well, she still has five minutes before the next event, Bob."

"What's that?"

"Any minute they'll be releasing the dog from the house. With any luck, he'll head straight for the brook, ignore Beckerman's calls, and romp through the muddy waters."

"Yesterday, I believe, he actually made it all the way to

the pile of mulch before Beckerman was able to grab him, hose him down, and get him back inside."

"Yes, Bob. That was certainly an exciting event."

"But today looks promising. There will be workmen at the house, painting the deck and fence. Beckerman will have a challenge keeping the dog away from the men and the paint."

"Yes, remember the winter games when the dog ran through the wet concrete subfloor Beckerman was laying down during the Kitchen Renovation competition?"

"Yup, that was something. Oh, here comes the dog! He's in the brook. Beckerman is throwing doggie treats at him but he's not responding and... whoa! The workmen just pulled up! The dog is out of the brook; he's running toward the workmen, and — *oh no!* He just lifted his muddy paws and jumped up on a workman!"

"She's going to lose points for that."

"Here comes Beckerman with the hose. She's got the dog by the collar, and... she sprays! That may be record time for her. She's toweling off the dog and... he's in the house. *The dog is in the house, folks!* A beautiful grab-spray-and-drag-the-dog performed by Beckerman."

"Okay, here come the numbers. 9.8, 9.7, 9.8, 9.9, 9.8. She pulled it off! Beckerman is still in the lead!"

"Wow, a very thrilling start to today's competition! We're going to break now for a commercial while Beckerman heads over to Dunkin' Donuts for a medium iced hazelnut coffee, and then it's the Algae Scrubbing event in the Pool Cleaning competition when we return.

"You're watching the Suburban Summer Olympics on NBC!"

Family Means Never
Having to Say
You're Crazy

King of the Grill

Like most couples, my husband and I have a fairly equitable division of household chores: I do the food shopping, make the meals, do the laundry, drop off and pick up the dry-cleaning, take care of the animals, make the beds, and clean the house. He takes the garbage down to the end of the driveway once a week. I'm not complaining because he is the breadwinner and I'm the stay-at-home mom, and the house stuff comes with my job description. Still, I'm very appreciative when he offers to pitch in and help out in some department. Typically this surge in volunteerism happens in the summer, and the area he likes to help out with is the cooking or, more specifically, the grilling.

Yes, folks, it's time to throw another shrimp on the barbie. Grill season has arrived and my husband, Super Grill Man, is back to save the world, one charcoal briquette at a time.

For Super Grill Man, grilling is a very, very serious business. So what if he can't find the on/off switch on the toaster oven? Grill Man knows that a real superhero only cooks on something with super-big burners, a rotisserie, and lots of BTUs. And while it's fine for us ladies to use utensils when we cook, when the fellas grill, they have to use *tools*. These tools are extra big and extra heavy and made of some kind of super indestructible alloy from another planet to protect Super Grill Man from the searing heat of the grill, as well as from any dastardly villains who may be lurking about, looking to steal his barbeque sauce. And because every superhero needs not only his special tools, but also something to carry them in on that long, treacherous walk from the kitchen to the back deck, the tools also come in their own monogrammed, triple-locked, titanium case.

It is always a big event when Grill Man handles dinner. First there is the closely-guarded *marinading of the meat,* which is followed by the much-anticipated *lighting of the grill.* Next, of course, is the actual *grilling of the food,* with special attention paid to moving the meat to strategic locations on the grill surface for optimal blackening. Finally we have the *serving of the food;* a red carpet presentation of the charcoaled meal by Grill Man to the grateful, humble, and starving family members at the table.

Although Grill Man usually only handles one-fourth of the actual meal while we mere mortals make the salad, potatoes, and vegetables in the lowly kitchen, somehow it ends up being everyone's belief that Grill Man has single-handedly prepared the meal. Thus he is rewarded with cheers and applause as he carries the burnt offering to the table. Clearly, he does deserve this praise, for he has stood at his post, diligently and without wavering for at least ten minutes while the flames licked at his wrists and the smoke burned his eyes just so his family could enjoy this selfless act of grilling love.

There are times, of course, when he must abandon his post to the unfortunately timed call of nature or the even less fortunately timed call from his mother. It is then, in a blink, that grilling perfection is snatched from his grasp and we end up having charred rocks for dinner.

As we all survey the inedible chunks of blackened food, Grill Man suddenly transforms from his superhero persona to his human alter ego, my husband.

"Is there any lasagna left over from last night?" he asks.

"Absolutely," I tell him supportively.

"Super."

Shake, Rattle, and Roll

M y older brother, a doctor, lives in Los Angeles. For the life of me, I cannot understand the appeal of what those who are hipper-than-thou refer to as the "Left Coast."

Growing up in a suburb of New York, the most exciting thing that ever happened was probably the day the local pizza joint owner torched his own restaurant to collect the insurance, never guessing that he might be arrested for arson.

Since my brother moved out to L.A., he's lived through wildfires and mudslides that almost wiped out his medical practice, earthquakes that nearly demolished his condo, and enough riots, beatings, and post-trial uprisings that one could almost long for the days of Marshall law.

I know New York City is no paradise. But there, at least, Mother Nature isn't one of the FBI's 10 Most Wanted, and the only time we got close to a citywide uprising was when they threatened to do away with rent control.

Still, as a doctor with celebrity patients, my brother gets to hobnob with the rich and pseudo-famous, and I suppose that could be fun. However, his hobnobbing usually takes place while examining an inflamed boil, bunion, or some other unglamorous irritated edifice or appendage. On the upside, he does get to go to the Oscars and film screenings and gets house seats to his patients' sold-out plays, while *my* biggest claim to fame is once having met Dr. Ruth. But is it really worth sitting in freeway traffic for two hours to go five miles just for the thrill of clearing up a movie star's eczema?

And yet he will still call me on the nastiest day of the East Coast winter to boast that while we are shivering and shoveling, he is sitting outside in his hot tub sipping a margarita.

"Your city is going to hell in a hand basket and you're excited because it's sunny and 75° in December?" I ask him.

"Yup," he answers. "Wait, hold on a sec."

Thirty seconds later he comes back on the phone.

"Sorry. It was just a small aftershock."

Aftershock?

I try to like L.A., really I do. But every time I go out there it's like, totally, you know, kind of not my scene, fer sure.

Aside from my apprehension about being in the middle of Mother Nature's real-life amusement park, I often feel like an alien visitor from another planet. There I am, a moderately sized, closely shorn brunette, in a sea of willowy six-foot blonds on rollerblades. So much do I stand out, a satellite camera could pick me out from orbit without even zooming in.

And then there's the food. Where I come from, pizza comes in two forms: thin and crispy, plain or pepperoni, from places called John's or Joe's or Ray's or Original Ray's (no relation to Ray's, I'm told). With all the New Yorkers who move to L.A. pretending to be native Californians, I figured there must be pizza somewhere in L.A. So, on my last trip to L.A., after a week of sushi had left my mercury levels in the upper stratosphere, my brother finally acquiesced and took me out for pizza.

Hooray, I thought, something I can relate to. But at the California pizza place, I had choices like Seafood Supreme pizza with calamari and clams, or Smoked Turkey with Brie pizza.

"Do you have any pepperoni?" I asked our waiter.

He gave me a smug look. "You must be from New York."

"You must be an out-of-work actor," I replied.

"Why don't you call Domino's in New York?" he snapped. "I'm sure they'll deliver."

With a sniff, I got back in my rented convertible and drove the half-mile back to my brother's condo, because nobody walks in L.A. With all the traffic on the freeway, it took us an hour to get home.

"Tell me again why you like it out here," I asked him.

"It never snows in southern California," he sang to me.

True. It quakes. It burns. It floods. It slides into the Pacific Ocean. But it never snows.

Would You Like Some Toile
with That Jacquard?

Like many women I know, everything I've learned about the finer points of home decorating comes from a magazine or HGTV. This sum of knowledge would be defined as "not much," but it's still a heck of a lot more than my husband knows. Since we're still in that early childhood, "don't spend money on furniture because the kids will destroy it" stage, the topic of décor doesn't really come up all that much. But occasionally I get the bug to spruce the place up. When that happens, my husband and I have trouble speaking the same language.

"I think we need some window treatments in here," I said, eyeballing our naked family room windows from where we sat on the couch watching TV.

"What do they need to be treated with?" he asked.

I stared at him. "Window treatments are curtains."

"Then call them curtains."

I felt a twitch starting in my eye and decided to change the subject.

"Do you like this duvet?" I asked, showing him a picture from a bedding catalog.

"What's a duvet?"

"It's like a sheet that covers the quilt."

"Why don't you just get a quilt that you like instead of getting one you have to cover?"

"You just *don't*," I said in exasperation. "What about this duvet?"

"It's okay," he said, glancing over from the TV.

"How about this one?" I asked, turning the page.

"It looks like the other one."

"How can you say that? This one is a toile and the other is a jacquard!"

He looked at me. "I don't understand a word you just said."

I decided to make the decision on my own and save myself the brain embolism I knew I would have if the conversation continued.

Most married men I know have risen above the bean-bag chair stage of decorating known as Early American Bachelor Pad and have learned to appreciate furniture that doesn't come with built-in cup holders. But they are still happy to let their wives take the lead in the decorating department. My husband is no exception. While he does have an opinion about the furniture and paint colors and tiles, he will be the first to admit he can't tell the difference between aubergine and eggplant, and why the hell don't they just call it purple, anyway?

Still, he is usually supportive when I want to make small changes around the house, and will even go so far as to suggest some upgrades when he feels we need them.

Realizing I was itching for some home improvement,

he took me aside one day and told me we had a little extra money to buy some furniture for the living room.

"What kind of furniture?" I asked.

"I don't know. Maybe some sofas and a new coffee table."

I started fantasizing about a Queen Anne chair, a skirted, rolled-arm sofa, and a leather ottoman coffee table.

"Great! How much money are we talking about?"

"Oh, about a thousand dollars."

"*A thousand dollars?*" I shrieked.

"Yeah," he said enthusiastically. "What do you think?"

"A thousand dollars," I repeated. "Are you kidding? That's not a living room set. That's a *chair!*"

"Fine," he said. "But for a thousand dollars, that chair better have a cup holder."

The Handy Husband

Here's something I don't understand: There are some guys who seem to have a natural ability for fixing things, and some who don't. Yet, take a guy who has absolutely no aptitude for home improvement, stick him in Home Depot, and he becomes convinced that with a wrench and some lug nuts, he can repair just about anything in the house.

Why is this? I certainly have no misconceptions that, say, dressing me in designer clothing will make me a model, that watching HGTV will make me an interior designer, or that singing in the shower will qualify me to be on *American Idol*. Well, okay, maybe that last one.

To be fair, my husband is not without some sense of how to make minor repairs. But he insists on trying to fix things he can't, gets frustrated, and gives up after there's a hole in the wall the size of North Dakota. Then he calls the handyman to fix the original problem, as well as the one he created. The funny thing is, when he can't accomplish what he set out to do, he always blames it on the tools.

"I can't do this," he says. "I don't have the right molly."

I don't know who Molly is, but if my husband knew what he was doing, why didn't he get the right tool when he bought the other fifty dollars' worth of stuff for the job?

I mean, the *handyman* never has the wrong molly, right?

Then there's the always popular "This is a much bigger job than I thought it was." Something tells me the handyman would have known that there was a beam behind the wall before he started drilling.

Because of my husband's aborted attempts at home repairs, we now not only have a hole in the wall that we didn't have before, we have to live with it for another month because the guy we could have called to fix it right away is on another job and won't be available for several weeks.

Honestly, I don't blame my husband. He means well. I blame the hardware store. There's something about a hardware store, especially a really big one, that makes a guy become deluded with imagined home-repair superpowers. He sees all these big shiny tools and some smiling guy in a nice red apron approaches to help. No matter the job, the guy says, "Oh sure, all you need is this, this, and that. No problem." Of course they say that, they want to sell stuff. This never happens when I go shopping in the department store, for say, makeup. I almost *never* walk out with foundation, mascara, eye shadow, and an entire facial cleansing system I don't need, because the cheap stuff I bought at the drugstore works just fine. Well, almost never.

And I certainly never undertake a home improvement project I can't complete just to save money. At least not since the time I decided to lay down a new kitchen floor while my husband was out of town. Who knew you're not supposed to clean out the bucket of subfloor solution in

Tracy Beckerman

the kitchen sink because it will harden in your garbage disposal? Or that you shouldn't spraypaint a kitchen table in the garage below 72° because the paint will bubble and set that way? Or that Liquid Plumber should never be used in a dishwasher?

Okay, so maybe I'm guilty of doing the same thing. But where do you think I got the idea that I could do it myself?

Actually, my idea was that I could do it better.

Now we have two holes in the wall.

Anyone know a good handyman?

Quoth the Bridesmaid, "Nevermore!"

O ne of the perks of being out of my twenties is that most of my friends, like me, are finally married. Therefore I am done with that awful rite of passage known as "The Bridesmaid."

Yes, it was always an honor to be asked to be in a friend's wedding. But was it an honor to be asked to wear a hideous dress? I don't think so.

Not that the brides ever thought it was hideous. Time and again they would swear that they were going to pick out pretty bridesmaid dresses. And then there I would be on the wedding day, wearing something in the teal or fuchsia family, a bow across my butt and taffeta as far as the eye could see.

"After the wedding, you can cut it down and wear it as a cocktail dress," the future bride would assure me. I tried this once. I went to a cocktail party looking like a bridesmaid in a tutu.

The only excuse I can think of for these usually fashion-forward women selecting fabrics and colors that shouldn't even be used to frame windows is temporary, wedding-induced insanity.

Or maybe the ugly-gown tradition came about as a way to ensure that the bride was the most beautiful woman at the wedding. Even the plainest bride looks stunning when she's surrounded by women in tragically ugly dresses.

It's the same philosophy as sitting next to an overweight woman on the beach so you look thinner.

Having worn my share of god-awful bridesmaid dresses, I took pity on my bridesmaids and told them to buy any dress they liked as long as it was white. Did the girls in my wedding party match? Not really. Were they happy because they didn't look like the Von Trapp Family Singers at my wedding? You bet! Unfortunately, most of my friends fell into that wedding-induced insanity category when they got married themselves.

For one friend's wedding (name withheld to protect the guilty), we were told that the bridesmaid dresses would be custom-made, which gave me hope. That is, until the future bride informed me that the largest size the gowns could be made in was a ten with a C-cup bra. Having just given birth to my second child, I could barely fit into a size foutrteen, let alone a ten, and nursing had me busting out of a double-D.

"Do you think you could lose weight by the wedding?" inquired the future bride.

Oh, no problem. Three months to lose twenty pounds and fit into a size ten dress, even though I was a size twelve before I got pregnant? For you, babe, anything.

Then there were the shoes. We could choose a $150 pair of feet-pinchers or a $300 pair. I figured since my feet were going to hurt either way, I'd save the money.

"After you buy them, send the shoes to me so I can get them all dyed in the same dye lot," she told the twelve of us. As if anyone would have noticed if the shades were different — the dresses were floor-length.

We were told, not asked, to wear the same brand and shade of lipstick, nail polish, and eye shadow, and to show up at the reception hall hours before the wedding to have our hair put up in a French twist by a guy from a big-name salon who would charge us $200 an hour.

Through it all, I uttered nary a peep of protest to the bride, although I muttered quite a bit under my breath.

Finally, the big day arrived, with all twelve of us looking like Barbie bridesmaids, resplendent in aubergine, and me stuffed into a size ten-dress like a trussed-up Thanksgiving turkey. However, when the time came for the bridal-party portraits, the bride took so long to get ready that they had to skip the pictures and move straight to the ceremony.

Nonetheless, five hours later, they were married, off on their honeymoon, and I was breathing a huge sigh of relief.

Until the phone rang three months later.

"I decided I want to have the wedding portraits taken," said the former bride. "I paid for them and I want them, so can you get dressed exactly the way you looked at the wedding and come to the reception hall for pictures?"

I smiled as I looked in the mirror at my newly shorn crew cut.

"I'll be right over."

Why I Would Make a Lousy Man

As a spokeswoman for my gender, I have to say: this Men are from Mars, Women are from Venus thing is not without its validity.

Certainly, there are many differences for which I am grateful. Who, if not my husband, would fearlessly rid my home of spiders, mice, and UCBs (unidentified crawling bugs) as I cower on a club chair nearby? Who would program the DVD player, fix the DVD player, and shop for a new DVD player when the old one gives up the ghost? Who would change all the burned-out lightbulbs, take out the smelly garbage, remember to get the oil changed in the car, negotiate with the gardeners, clean the icky things out of the pool filter, and let the kids ride around on his back when I'm way too tired to play horsey?

Yeah, him.

I try to remember all these things when I find a pair of his shoes in every room in the house. When I tell him to meet me someplace at 6 p.m. and he's sure I said 6:30. When my honey-do list goes undone for months on end. Or when he gives me the "day off" and takes care of the kids (he does get points for that), but I arrive home to find the sink full of dishes, the beds unmade, and so much disarray that it takes me two hours to return it to how it was when I left.

"We had a lot of fun today," he tells me as I dustbust bits of mac and cheese off the kitchen floor.

"Couldn't you have fun and still do the dishes and the other chores on your list?" I ask.

"How could I pick up the dry-cleaning if I'm taking care of the kids?"

And therein lays the root of the problem. It's what scientists call the *multi-tasking gene*. It's quite active in the X-chromosome, but the presence of a Y-chromosome will render it virtually impotent. (I realize impotent is not a good word to use around Martians, but it's true.)

For example, I can simultaneously make dinner, bathe the kids, fold the laundry, and talk on the phone without breaking a sweat. (There should be an Olympic category for this.)

He can do all of those things. But not even two at the same time.

To his credit, he gives me kudos for accomplishing all this and thanks me profusely for picking up his dry-cleaning, making him a nice dinner, and keeping the kids alive for another day, all while I endeavor to have a part-time writing career.

And to be fair, I know there are things about us Venus chicks that drive men crazy, too. It completely befuddles my husband that I can keep the house immaculate while the inside of the car routinely looks like there was a fast-food explosion. He has no idea why I move his piles of papers, receipts, magazines, etc. off the desk and out of sight and then forget where I stuffed them. And he really can't understand what all the fuss is about if there's garbage in the garbage can (isn't that what it's there for?), mud on the doormat (isn't that what it's there for?), or dirty clothes piled up on the chair in the bedroom (he admits I have him on that one).

In the grand scheme of things, are these gender-related differences really such a big deal? On a bad day, sure, it can really get my goat. But I need to remember, here's a guy who went out at 3 a.m. to get me nasal spray when I had a horrendous cold and couldn't sleep; who told me it wasn't a big deal, "the important thing is no one got hurt" when I backed out of the garage and ripped the front bumper off the new car; and who woke for 2 a.m. feedings, changed nasty diapers without flinching, and taught the kids how to swim, ride bicycles, and tie shoelaces, all with the patience of a saint.

And when he comes home at 8 p.m., and we've both had it, he reads the kids a story, hears about their day, and puts them to bed.

Does it really matter that Martians can't do the dishes and take care of the kids at the same time?

No.

Well, maybe just *one* dish.

"We're back in New Providence for the 2004 Suburban Summer Olympics, where local favorite Tracy Beckerman has returned for a fourth consecutive summer to try to bring home the gold. So, what do we have on tap for today, Allison?"

"Well, Bob, in this morning's Kitchen Renovation event, Beckerman will be competing in the Women's Refrigerator Delivery and Installation category. She did very well in the preliminaries, coming in second overall in the Freestyle Refrigerator Selection event."

"Yes, Allison, but it was pretty touch-and-go for awhile there. If you recall, one of the judges initially disqualified her from the event when she appeared to make an illegal turn from the Kenmore model to a SubZero."

"That's true. But when we looked at the instant replay, it was obvious that she was in bounds, and she was reinstated into the competition."

"Close call for Beckerman."

"Yes, Bob, but she handled it like the champion she is. Now we're on to the main event. Beckerman confirmed delivery this morning and had a plumber shut off the main water valve just a few minutes ago."

"Hold on, Allison. The delivery truck has just pulled up. Beckerman is running outside to inspect the refrigerator and… oh no, the dog! The dog is out the door and he's headed straight for the deliverymen."

"Oh, too bad! If he jumps up on them she'll lose valuable points. If you remember, last year she was almost disqualified for the exact same thing when she had workmen painting her fence."

"I do remember. Whoa, look at that. The deliverymen must have been standing right near the dog's electric fence. A warning alarm went off as the dog approached, and he ran back into the house with his tail between his legs."

"Very smart of Beckerman to have added that element to her routine this summer, Bob."

"Okay, the refrigerator is in the house and the workmen are disconnecting the water hose from the old fridge. Holy cow! There's water pouring out of the hose! The valve was not shut off properly and water is flooding the kitchen! What a disaster!"

"But look at Beckerman, Bob. The deliverymen are just standing there stunned, but Beckerman has thrown open the kitchen window, grabbed the hose, and directed it out the window and into the garden. Very nice form!"

"What an incredible save of the newly laid tile floor!"

"Unbelievable! She's got towels down on the floor now and, wait, look at that… she's got the plumber in here. She kept him around just in case she had a problem. Brilliant move. The plumber has located the problem with the valve and the water has been shut off."

"Okay, Allison, the new refrigerator is installed and she's tipped the deliverymen. Here come the numbers. 9.8, 9.6, 9.7, 9.7, 9.8. Wow, that puts Beckerman back in the lead! You can see she's very excited. She just hugged the plumber!"

"Yuck! We'll be back for the next event, the Laundry Triathalon, right after these messages!"

Wagging the Dog

Life Is Ruff

The minute my son turned seven, he reminded us this was the year we had promised to A) take him and his sister to Disney World, B) teach him and his sister how to ski, and C) get a dog.

Somewhere in my naïve 30-something mind, I had figured five and seven were the perfect ages for all of the aforementioned activities. I just hadn't realized that I'd set them all up to happen the same year.

Surrendering ourselves to the inevitable, we researched breeds, selected a breeder, and made first contact. In my naïve 30-something mind I had figured we call, we pick out a puppy, bada-bing, bada-boom, we bring home a dog. How hard could it be?

In reality, that's how it works when you *adopt* a dog. When you *buy* a dog, you have to go through a process similar to becoming a naturalized citizen of the United States.

First there was the phone interview. After passing that, I was allowed to fill out a questionnaire, complete with pet history, personal references, and how I thought we could achieve world peace. Finally there was the in-person interview. I dressed nicely and palmed doggie treats for the pups. We were approved.

It wasn't this hard to refinance our mortgage.

I suppose we could have adopted an abandoned or unwanted dog from a shelter. But with two young kids in the house, I wanted to ensure we brought in a pet with the best possible disposition toward children.

At last the time came. The puppy was eight weeks old, and we were all so excited we could have just peed in our pants. (Fortunately, we already had plenty of wee-wee pads in the house in case that happened).

As we counted down the days and shared our enthusiasm with everyone we met, I was somewhat surprised by the number of people who pooh-poohed on my puppy parade.

"You do know there's going to be dog hair *everywhere?*"

"You do know he's going to pee all over the house?"

"You do know he's going to chew on *everything?*"

"You do know you have to be near home all the time to feed him and walk him — you can't just pick up and leave for weekends any time you want?"

"No, wait," I said. "You mean dogs shed? Puppies pee and chew? They have to be fed and walked??? Oh my God, I didn't know that!!!"

These are the same people who, when I told them I was pregnant years earlier, had said, "You'll never sleep again… you'll be changing diapers for years… you'll never be able to just pick up and go away for weekends!"

Of course I knew a dog would be a lot of work. And there would be a lot of hair. And some furniture would be gnawed on. But I choose to focus not on the negatives, but on all the joy and love this pet would bring into our family. Kind of like when my husband and I decided to have children.

I wish more people could have responded like my friend Ed. When I announced our decision to get a dog, he broke out in a terrific grin, gave me a huge bear hug and said, "Oh, I'm so happy for you!"

Ed, who shares his home with two wonderful golden retrievers, knows all about the responsibilities of dog ownership. But for him, the cup is half-filled with puppy chow, the grass is green enough, and his life is richer because of these two dogs.

Hmmm. *Two* dogs...?

Adventures in Puppyland

Now I know why they make puppies so cute. It's so when they pee on the floor, chew the tassels off your rug, and howl all night, you don't throw them out the window. (Of course I wouldn't do that! Shame on you for thinking it!)

Yes, we are in Puppyland. In Puppyland, you don't sleep because the puppy misses his littermates and howls at night. In Puppyland, you take him outside to do his business at 4:30 in the morning while you are freezing in your jammies, and he doesn't go until you're back in the house. Then he immediately goes on the floor. In Puppyland, he ignores all the chew toys you spent a small fortune on in favor of your rattan chair, your daughter's boots, and the place in the kitchen where the linoleum is peeling up from the floor.

So yes, I'm tired, my house is a wreck, and my daughter's boots are history. But our puppy, Riley, is so darn cute, we forgive him because we chose to live in Puppyland. And because we can't stand to hear everyone say, "I told you so."

We started with one book on how to train a puppy. Six days later, we owned a whole library on the subject. They all say the same thing, but we keep buying more in the hope that one of them will unlock the secret to housebreaking, crate-training, and boot-chewing. The problem, I realized, is that we speak two different languages, Riley and I. (This is something I learned from Gary Larson.) I say, "Riley, no biting. Riley, go potty — no, Riley, not *there,* outside! Come on, Riley." But Riley hears, "Riley, blah blah. Riley, blah blah — blah, Riley, blah *blah,* blah! Blah blah, Riley." Thus, until he adds more words to his repertoire, all the books in the world are not worth as much as the mounds of paper towels I've been buying to clean up his messes.

The good news is, with patience and perseverance, I should spend far less time cleaning up puppy pee than I did changing my two children's diapers. But it's hard to remember that Puppyland is a temporary residence when I leave the dog in the car for a minute because I forgot something inside, and return to find that he has taken a bath in the remains of the cold hazelnut coffee that I had left on the dashboard. A dog could smell of worse things than hazelnut, though, so I chalk it up to carelessness on my part, towel him off, and move on.

To compensate for the challenges, there are many good things about having a puppy. (Give me a minute, I'll think of them.) No, seriously, he has inspired my children to hang up their coats and put away their shoes when they get home, lest their clothing end up as puppy chow. Playing with the dog has replaced playing with the PlayStation as the kids' favorite activity. And there is nothing, I repeat nothing, that beats a sleeping puppy in your lap when you're relaxing in front of the TV at night.

From what I understand, we are quite lucky. As far as puppies go, Riley is really quite mellow, not overly aggressive, and not a manic chewer. After only six days, he responded to his name, and tries to let us know much of the time when he has to go out, albeit with only about six seconds' notice. We had only three nights of plaintive howling before he settled down and started to sleep in his crate. And he is a loveable mass of wriggling fur who, when scooped up in your arms, will cover your face and ears with warm, slobbering kisses.

Yes, we love this new addition to our family — peeing, chewing, howling, and all. And when I'm inclined to forget this, all it takes is a giant grin from a passerby to remind me.

"Oh, he's soooo cute. Can I pick him up?" asks a woman walking by.

"Sure," I say.

"Oh, I just love that puppy smell, don't you? What *is* it?"

"Hazelnut."

Sit, Stay, and Buy
Me Something Shiny

My puppy starts obedience school this week, and I couldn't be happier.

"Thank God," I told my mother as I cleaned up another puddle in the kitchen. "With any luck, in eight weeks I will have a dog who comes when I call him, sits, lies down, and stays on command."

Which got me thinking: Wouldn't it be great if they had obedience school for kids? An eight-week program would teach such basics as "make your bed," "get dressed," "go to sleep," and "eat what I put in front of you." Then maybe you could do an extended obedience program that taught more complex commands such as "no whining," "don't hit your brother (sister)," "turn off the TV," and "do your homework." All that for less than the price of a PlayStation 3, with results achieved well before college.

But why limit this to kids? How about an obedience school for husbands? The basic eight-week program would cover such necessities as "do the dishes," "take out the garbage," and "put your socks in the hamper." An additional program would have husbands responding positively to such commands as "give me the credit card, I'm going shoe shopping," "bathe the kids and put them to bed while I lounge on the sofa and do my nails," and "let's go see that new chick flick tonight."

The possibilities give me goose bumps.

I'm sure my husband would like an obedience program for wives. Forget mundane commands like "pick up the dry cleaning." his school would covers things like, "could you wear something sexy to bed tonight instead of that ratty old t-shirt?", "could we have something for supper besides spaghetti?", and "let's go see that mindless new action film starring that aging actor who's too old to be doing this, and that model-turned-actress who couldn't act her way out of a paper bag."

Oh yeah, he would loooove that! But this is my fantasy, so we'll move on.

Just as people with driving violations go to traffic school, I would love to be able to send rude people to manners school. The guy who repeatedly tries to sneak 20 groceries in the Ten Items or Less line; the lady who swoops in and takes the parking spot you've been waiting for at the mall; the person who snorts and huffs and sighs when he's waiting for you to finish paying for something but it's not your fault because the debit card machine isn't working. Yeah, those people. Send 'em off to obedience school and teach them "no extra groceries," "no stealing spots," and "no impatient, huffy noises!"

I'd like to see schools that teach garbagemen not to dump half the garbage in my driveway when emptying the cans into the truck; schools that teach inconsiderate parents not to send their coughing, sneezing, typhoid-carrying kids to my house for a playdate; and a school that teaches dog owners that the island in the middle of my street's cul-de-sac is not exempt from the pooper-scooper law.

Yes, this would certainly make life nice and easy. But I suppose I would miss out on all the rewards of achieving the same results through my own communication skills. Not that I'm a big fan of confrontation. But there's something to be said for working out your own problems.

So one day after contemplating all this, I ran into a friend.

"Where are you off to?" he asked.

"Obedience school."

"Oh really," he said. "Is your husband sending you?"

Apparently, we need an obedience school for wise-cracking friends as well.

How Much Dog Can a Woodchuck Chuck?

When we were trying to decide what kind of pet to get, one of the reasons we opted for a dog was to give me a little more security when my husband was away. That said, I could never claim to have gotten my dog, Riley, for protection. True, he does have a mean bark, but the only reason someone might fear him is if they were afraid of being slobbered to death. Still, I like to think that if I were in some kind of mortal danger, he would rise to the occasion and come to my rescue, like Lassie or Benji or Underdog. The unfortunate truth, however, is that when the going gets tough, it's every man, woman, and dog for themselves.

I learned this the day I came home from running errands and let Riley out to do his business. He had just gotten started when suddenly the fur on his shoulders stood up and he bolted to the side of our deck, out of my view.

As I walked to the edge of the deck, I heard barking followed by a mean growl that was decidedly not dog language. There, nose-to-nose with my dog, was the biggest woodchuck I'd ever seen. I didn't even know they came that big. This one was like a gopher on steroids, an uber-woodchuck, something from the future when rodents take over the world. I half expected it to whip out an Uzi and take out all the squirrels in the neighborhood.

But no. It simply raised a paw and took a swipe at my dog's nose. Riley stopped barking and jumped back in surprise.

"Riley, *Riley!* Come! Come here now!" Usually Riley is so stubborn, I could be holding a filet mignon and he wouldn't come when I called him until *he* felt like it. But now he looked at me out of the corner of his worried eye and slowly backed up, while the monster woodchuck stayed frozen, its paw raised as if to say, "One false move, Rover, and I'm gonna make dog chow outta you."

I called the dog again, and this time he ran to me. But when Riley moved, the woodchuck suddenly broke formation and started to run after the dog, who was running right to me. I did the only thing I could think of: I turned and ran too.

Picture this: an extremely large rodent chasing a medium-sized dog chasing an average-sized woman, across the cedar deck of a suburban home.

You can't make this stuff up.

And to think, when I lived in the city, I was afraid of rats! Ha!

It was at this moment that the dog betrayed me. I had left the back door open, and as the dog and I ran screaming — well, actually, I was the only one screaming — with the crazy woodchuck hot on our heels, Riley caught up to me and pushed me out of the way to get to safety.

So much for man's best friend.

Two steps behind him, I dove into the house and slammed the door. As the dog and I panted on one side of the glass door and the woodchuck glared (if a woodchuck can glare) on the other, I turned to Riley and said, "Thanks a lot, you big scaredy-cat."

Then, with the safety of the two-inch-thick glass between them, Riley the Ferocious started barking and jumping at the door.

"Let me at him! I can take him! I'll tear him limb from limb!" he cried, or so I believe.

The woodchuck turned and waddled away, back to his giant woodchuck lair, probably right under my deck. Riley turned and padded away to his own lair on the family-room rug, and went to sleep.

I went into the kitchen and pulled out the Yellow Pages.

I wonder if there's such a thing as an attack cat.

The Battle of the Canine Bulge

According to a recent report by the National Research Council, one-fourth of our nation's pets are overweight. Apparently, now even dogs have to worry about bathing suit season. Not that I've caught my dog, Riley, staring in the mirror agonizing over the size of his thighs, but when the vet told me Riley was a couple of pounds overweight, I felt for him.

"We have to do something about Riley's weight," I told my husband. "We don't want him to feel insecure around thinner dogs."

Clearly, I have my own weight issues.

Since I am the person who feeds the dog, I felt somehow responsible for his extra poundage. But I soon realized it wasn't his meals that were the problem, but rather what he was eating in between.

On many occasions I have caught him helping himself to the kids' abandoned Happy Meals at the table. And their mac and cheese. And their hot dogs. Perhaps, I thought, I should change what I'm feeding the kids. Not that I don't provide them with healthier fare most of the time. But Riley is just as happy to steal the remains of my grilled chicken, pan-seared snapper, and vegetable lasagna as well.

So we started clearing the table right after dinner.

Then I caught him licking the dirty plates out of the dishwasher.

After researching the problem, I learned that dogs are binge eaters. Riley seems to be more of an indiscriminate eater than a binger. Does a ball of yarn have a lot of calories? Because he ate one of those. He's eaten half of my son's collection of rubber insects. He's bitten off and ingested most of the limbs of my daughter's wooden dolls, as well as two kitchen table legs and a dozen supposedly indestructible chew toys.

We soon realized that the contents of our house had become a veritable dog buffet, and we began cleaning up and closing doors on a regular basis. If nothing else, the dog had certainly improved our family's messy habits.

We thought we'd nicked the problem. But when we brought him to the vet, we found out he was still tipping the scales.

"Does he get a lot of treats?" asked the vet.

"Well, yeah," I answered sheepishly. "But in obedience training, they taught us to motivate the dog with food. A treat after he potties. A treat when he sits on command. When he comes. When he stays." I realized that all the treats were probably adding up to the equivalent of a third meal.

I checked in about the treat issue with a friend of mine who had taken the class with me.

"Don't you remember? We were supposed to wean them off the treats," she said. No, I didn't remember. Probably because we weren't in obedience school long before Riley had to drop out for emergency stomach surgery after eating the aforementioned ball of yarn and developing a bowel obstruction.

So I cut out the treats. He responded by eating my laptop manual. I let him run loose in the backyard three times a day for exercise. He responded by eating rocks from my garden. I took him for runs in the park. He ate mud.

I said to my husband, "I think Riley's father was a goat."

Finally I brought him back to the vet and we dumped him on the scale. I held my breath.

"Riley's weight is down," she said. "Good job!"

Yeah, good job for him. But the whole ordeal had stressed me out so much that I put on five pounds.

Hey, *someone* had to finish the kids' Happy Meals.

Barking up the Wrong Laundry Basket

There's a new device on the market that supposedly can translate your dog's barks. I have no idea if this thing works or not, but personally, I think it's a big waste of money. Any dog owner worth his weight in puppy chow knows exactly what his dog's woofs, whines, and yelps mean without a pricey contraption to spell it out for him.

For instance, when my dog, Riley, runs to the back door (which is glass) and barks like a dog possessed, he's not saying, "Let me out, nature calls." What he's really saying is, "Oh, I see a squirrel! Let me at him so I can show him who's boss." The bathroom request is much more subtle. He sits by the back door and looks at me forlornly as if to say, "If you know what's good for your carpet, you'll let me out soon."

We have a book on canine behavior that professes to know what my dog's nonverbal behavior means. (How I wish they had one of these for husbands. But that's another column.) According to the authors, when Riley licks my hand, he is acknowledging that I am the leader of the pack. But I know that it really means there were some traces of peanut butter on my fingers from making my son's lunch.

When Riley lies under the table during dinner, my son says, "Oh, look, Riley wants to be with the family." I know better. He's actually setting himself up for easy access when pieces of the kids' food inevitably fall onto the floor.

The dog may bark at squirrels, but when it comes to food, he's no dummy.

He will also let me know if I don't get him his breakfast fast enough. When I come down to the kitchen in the morning, if I try to make myself a cup of coffee before feeding him, he will stand and bark at me as if to say, "Hey, lady, I get two measly meals of dry kibble a day and I haven't eaten for 12 whole hours. Do you think you could wait five whole minutes for your stinkin' coffee so I could get some food around here???"

There is, however, one behavior that is an absolute mystery to me: he will sometimes bark at an overflowing laundry basket. Maybe the smell bothers him, although considering that he likes to chew on dirty socks, I don't think that's the case. Maybe he thinks there's a squirrel hiding under the pile, or perhaps an escaped lizard. He did, after all, locate a lost hamster under a pile of dirty laundry once, though I'm pretty sure that he stumbled upon it accidentally while looking for a dirty sock to chew on. Maybe the mound of dirty laundry simply scares him. I know it scares me. They say dogs are supposed to be empathetic to their owners' feelings, so maybe he just feels my pain about doing the laundry.

Still, I don't think this one question will keep me up at night. I'm not even curious enough to spend $99.95

on some gadget to translate his bark and solve the great laundry-basket mystery.

If they came up with something that could actually *teach* the dog to do the laundry... now that's something I would buy.

Interlude VII:
We Pause for a
Commercial Interruption

'Twas four weeks after Christmas and all through
the town
The lights and the wreaths were all coming down.
The shoppers had shopped, the gifts had gone back,
The bills from the credit cards were all in a stack.

The eggnog was gone, the tips had been tipped,
The gift to Aunt Millie had finally been shipped.
The lines at the mall were finally shorter
and holiday items went for two-and-a-quarter.

The children were safely all tucked in their beds
as visions of next Christmas danced in their heads.
More Barbies, more X-Men, more Pokemon, too.
And what would they do without Barney and Pooh?

Then from way up above there arose such a clatter.
My husband ran up to see what was the matter.
Someone was walking up there on the house,
And that someone was bigger for sure than a mouse.

A burglar? A reindeer? What could it be?
Something was headed straight for our chimney.

And then with an "oomf" and an "ugh" he came down,
Not through the chimney but down to the ground.
With big rosy cheeks and good cheer galore
Our mystery roof-walker appeared at the door.

"I'm the guy that you called, I'm a roofer named Kringle.
All that snow that just fell? It ruined your shingles.
You need a new roof," said the man dressed in red.
"If you don't do it soon it'll fall in on your head."

We looked at the children asleep in their beds,
At the pile of bills, and then scratched our heads.
Then we gave him a Visa to clean up the mess
Because Kringle won't take American Express.

Seasonal Psychosis

Germ Warfare

When Christmas has come and gone and the "50% Off All Holiday Items" signs sprout up in store windows, I know it's just a matter of time before the hum of "Jingle Bells" gives way to the unmistakable, undeniable sound of... sneezing.

I look at my son, from whom the offending sound just escaped, and I shudder. What's the big deal, right? It's just one little sneeze. But the next thing I know, everybody in my house is sick. And when the seven-year-old, his five-year-old sister, and the mom who wipes the runny noses are all sick at the same time, well... just shoot me.

When I had just one toddler, we spent most of our time at home, and we'd get one or two colds a season. But when my son went to kindergarten, we all entered a vast new unexplored germ pool. Suddenly every runny-nosed kid in his class became a little germ terrorist.

Soon the warning notes started coming home from school. A case of strep throat here, a pink eye there. Before I know it we've got the vaporizers running at full tilt, the counters are overflowing with Pediacare, and our house looks like we've won a contest in which first prize was a year's supply of tissues.

The worst part is not the coughing, dripping, and general yuckiness that infects our household for a week to ten days. Nor is it the inevitable ear infections that seem to follow each and every cold. It's not even the fact that I still have to be the great and wonderful mommy while I feel like my head's been stuffed with Play-doh. No, the worst part is the total boycott of my home by any and all of my friends with children. As long as my child's nose drips, I am a complete and utter pariah of parental society.

Not that I don't do the same thing to my friends when their kids are sick. But when the Kleenex is on the other nostril and you've been locked inside with the drippy duo for a week, you become desperate for the company of someone who doesn't whine and wheeze.

So first I tell a little lie. "Well, my son is getting over a cold and my daughter has a runny nose, but I think it's allergies."

They don't buy it. (Maybe it's the phlegmy, hacking cough they hear in the background while I'm on the phone.)

I call my second string of friends. It turns out their kids are sick too, and are probably the little darlings who got my kids sick in the first place.

Finally, just when I think it can't get any worse, my husband gets sick. It's not that I'm unfeeling. But he's worse than the two kids combined. The way he carries on, you'd think he'd just contracted double viral pneumonia while having a root canal without novocaine. Do I sympathize? Of course. I even make him a nice bowl of soup. Not home-made chicken soup, like (he informs me) his mother did when he was a kid, but regular old "if it's good enough for the kids, it's 'Um, um, good' enough for you" canned stuff.

A week to ten days later, my children healthy and my house germ-free, I call one of my friends to make a playdate and end my sentence of viral solitary confinement.

As she picks up the phone I hear a phlegmy, hacking cough in the background.

"My son is just getting over a cold and I think the baby has allergies," she tells me through stuffed nasal passages.

Yeah, right.

See you in March.

Ringing in the New Year... Quietly

There was a time when I felt like a loser with a capital "L" branded on my forehead if I didn't have some fabulous evening planned for New Year's Eve.

That was probably sometime before I had a husband, kids, and a bad case of sleep deprivation.

Stay up until midnight? What, are you kidding? The dog can stay up later than I can. Noisemakers? I have two kids for that. Champagne? I get enough bubbles in my Diet Coke after the kids shake the bottle vigorously before handing it to me.

But the pressure, the pressure! Not going out on New Year's Eve is like committing some kind of social blasphemy.

"What do you mean you're not going out for New Year's Eve?" one friend exclaimed in abject horror. "Are the kids sick? Did you recently have gum surgery?" She paused and raised an eyebrow. "Or weren't you invited to any parties?"

Not invited? Please! I may be blasphemous but I'm not a pariah.

We actually got a number of invitations this year:

"We're going to Times Square to see the ball drop," some wild and crazy friends informed us. "Come with us!"

Hmm, let's see. Stand around in sub-zero temperatures

with a million people for six hours so we can watch a big ball slide down a pole while we count backwards from ten. It's tempting, but I think I'll pass.

Another couple invited us to sit in their living room with them and watch the ball drop on TV. True, it would be warmer. But why fall asleep on their couch when I can fall asleep on my own?

"Let's go to a New Year's Eve dinner at a fabulous restaurant," suggested another friend. She then informed me that it cost $150 per person for a three-course dinner, including all the champagne you can drink. The catch was the restaurant had two seatings, at 7 p.m. and 9 p.m., which meant even if we went to the second seating and it took us an hour to eat, we would have spent $300 and still have two hours to kill before midnight.

Fun? Maybe. But it would be cheaper to get indigestion at home.

Don't get me wrong. I like a good celebration as much as the next person. I like it even more if it occurs early in the evening and I don't wake up with cotton-mouth the next morning. But I still feel like I owe everyone some big explanation if I decide to spend a quiet New Year's Eve at home with my husband in front of the fire, while the children are nestled all snug in their beds. We would rent a movie and, shockingly, we'd go to bed when we were tired, even if it meant having our midnight smooch at 10 p.m.

Sometimes I've lied in the past. "Sorry, we can't get a sitter." Or, "We'd love to come, but I just had earlobe surgery and I'm not up to it." And then there's the ever popular,

"Oh darn, we're going to be in Prague for New Year's."

But this year I decided honesty was the best policy.

"We're staying home, making a fire, eating Chinese food, and going to bed at 10," I told one devoted New Year's Eve-partying friend of mine.

A strange look came over her face. I thought for sure she was going to take me off her Christmas card list, or at the very least report me to the New Year's Eve Patheticness Patrol. But instead she said, "You know, that sounds great. Maybe we'll stay home this year, too."

Loser.

Post-Traumatic Snow Syndrome

Sometime around February I start to feel like Nanook of the North.

I realize I'm sick of the short, dark days, of my stinging, chapped lips, and of my hyperactive children who suffer from cold-weather-induced cabin fever. I cling to desperate hope that Punxatawny Phil, that shadow-phobic ground-hog with prophetic powers, will foresee an end to all that is snowy, white, and cold (as if an oversized rat could really predict the weather).

I remember the good old days when global warming meant a tepid winter, little to no snowfall, and just the tiniest bit of melting of the polar ice cap. Now we have something called El Niño, which, when it happens, means I'd better make an appointment with my chiropractor because I'm going to throw my back out shoveling lots of snow.

Thus, ski bunny that I'm not, I wait impatiently for winter to go its frigid way. That said, I am sane enough to realize that at the beginning of February, we cannot yet expect to see the light at the end of the wind tunnel.

So when my son lost his mittens sledding, I thought it was perfectly reasonable to trudge off to the mall to purchase a new pair. However, I think I might have inadvertently slept through the vernal equinox, because when I got to the mall, there were no mittens. There were no hats. There was no cold-weather wear anywhere. There were, in great abundance, shorts, t-shirts, and bathing suits. Sun hats and sunglasses. Sandals and sneakers. Halters and hot pants.

I know everyone is eager to get on with the next season, but let's think here. It's February. *February!* T-shirt season is a good three months away.

Soon I realized it wasn't just the clothing industry that was out of whack. The hardware store was having a clearance sale on snowblowers. At the ski shop, skiwear was 75% off. And at the drugstore, the Benadryl had been replaced by Bain de Soleil. The Cold-eze by Coppertone.

I didn't get it. Were these people living in the same time zone I was?

And it's not like such bizarre behavior is specific to *this* time of year. Were that the truth, we could chalk it up to sunlight deprivation or something. But I remember sometime last July, I desperately needed a new bathing suit and all I could find was one lone Speedo amidst a sea of down jackets and shearlings.

It's bad enough that the *retailers* are already pushing next season's must-haves on us. I actually have *friends* who are at the mall this minute buying their kids' spring wardrobes. It's like they're afraid it will turn 75 degrees overnight and their children will either have to wear (gasp!) last year's t-shirts for a day or go naked.

I guess if this phenomenon happened at the exact same time each year, I could gear up for it psychologically.

You know, buy some self-tanning cream, take my chaise out to the beach, and dig my toes into the, um, snow. The problem is that the stores are moving the seasonal switch up just a tiny bit earlier each year. Last year I remember looking for boots in February and finding only strappy sandals. This year, the stores brought out the flip-flops in January.

At first I thought this was a real problem. Then I realized if I waited long enough, things would right themselves. I figure if they keep moving the preseason stuff back a month each year, by 2010 the summer items will be selling in April, when they should be.

In the meantime, I plan to order my son some mittens from a clothing company in Australia. It's summer there now, so they probably have all their winter items well stocked.

My Flu Is Worse than Your Flu

I love those little sayings like *When it rains, it pours* and *Misery loves company*. These are just some of the phrases I heard from people while my two kids and I were home with the flu. Sympathy would have been welcome. Offers to loan us some new videos would have been a nice gesture. But idioms? I'm beginning to understand why idiom and idiot share the same first four letters. I think people say these things because they don't know what else to say. But if you're going to rub salt into my wound, why not be honest and just say, *Hey, better you than me.*

Then there are the people who think being sick is a great big competition. Apparently, *my* body aches, fever, stuffed head, and sore throat were a mere discomfort compared with what *they* have had to endure.

"You think *you're* sick? Last January I got the German-Asian-Galapagos-Swine Flu. My temperature was 107°, my tongue turned blue, and I couldn't get out of bed for a month."

Better still are those who are annoyed because my temporary sickness threatens to inconvenience them.

Me: "Hi. (Sniff.) It's Tracy."

Other Mom: "Oh, you don't sound so good."

Me: "Yeah, I'm sick and so are the kids. I have to cancel our playdate for tomorrow."

OM: "Gee, you don't sound *that* bad. When did the kids get sick? They're probably at the tail end of it. We can still get together!"

Me: "No, I don't think so. We all feel pretty lousy."

OM: "Hmmph. Well, I don't think I can get anyone to play at the last minute. This is a real problem. I'd better go... I have to make some calls and see if I can find someone else!"

And let us not forget the friends who aren't doctors, but think that motherhood qualifies them to dispense pharmaceutical advice. I have a brother who's an actual doctor and he doesn't give me unsolicited advice. My neighbor is also a doctor and I don't bother him with anything as mundane as the flu. Poison ivy, yes. Flu, no. If I were really miserable, these are the two people I might actually choose to consult, as well as (surprise, surprise) my own internist. Yet almost everyone who calls thinks they have the miracle cure for what ails me.

"The only thing that works is to take two Tylenol every four hours and alternate it with Advil, but not if you're also taking naproxen or anything with pseudo-hydro-chloro-something at the same time," said one pseudo-MD.

I'm pretty sure that if I followed this advice I would end up in a coma, so I usually opt instead for picking the right Robitussin for my symptoms and leaving it at that.

If I were still searching for sympathy, I might call my own mother. But for some reason, my misery often makes her nostalgic.

"I remember how tough it was when you kids were young and would get sick and I'd be sick, too. Of course your father would usually be away on a business trip so it was even harder for me."

I would cut her off before she could tell me how my brother caught the mumps right before they invented the vaccine, and how lucky I am because we have a vaccine for that and for measles and chicken pox. What all this has to do with the price of tea in China and my bout with the flu, I don't know, but it makes her feel like she's making me feel better, so what the heck.

The truth is, when I'm feeling lousy and the kids are sick at the same time, the only phone call I really appreciate is the one from my husband telling me he's on his way home from work.

That is just what the doctor ordered.

The Early Bird Gets the Game Boy

This is the time of year, when the first leaves start to fall, that my kids really begin to get excited about the holidays.

No, not Halloween. That would be the logical conclusion, considering it's October and the stores are filled with costumes and candy. And it's not Thanksgiving, the next holiday around the corner. No, my kids are already starting to plan for Hanukkah. Why shouldn't they? With only 66 shopping days left (five fewer days than Christmas, I might add), they want to make sure they get dibs in on every junky toy that looks phenomenal when advertised on TV during every commercial break on Nickelodeon.

I know the marketers are just doing their jobs. But is it really necessary to launch the attack this far in advance? I'm not really thinking about Christmas and Hanukkah toys when our pool is still open.

But my kids are.

"Mom, come here, *quick!*" a young voice beseeches me from the family room.

I hightail it in, imagining that one of my kids has sustained some mortal injury, only to find the older one waving frantically at the TV.

"Look, it's the new Game Boy Advance SP in titanium!" he announces dreamily. Not unlike the way my husband reacts when he sees a new sports car commercial, come to think of it.

"You just got a Game Boy Advance for Hanukkah last year," I remind him.

"No, this is the SP. The *sssssppppppp!* In titanium!"

"How is it different from the one you already have?" I ask him.

"I dunno," he shrugs. "It just looks really cool."

Ahh. The dreaded cool factor. I know I've already lost half the battle, so I decide to go online to see for myself.

The first thing I notice when I go to Amazon.com is not how cool the toy is, but how incredibly expensive it is. Call me crazy, but I think $199 for something that will probably break in the first ten minutes is a little extreme. And then I see, in the smallest possible print, that this particular model (in titanium!) is currently out of stock.

When will they get more in? It doesn't say. So I call my local Toys "R" Us, wait on hold for a millennium, and then find out that they are out of stock, too. Since I have a real person on the phone, I ask when they're getting more in.

"I'm not sure," responds the well-informed employee whose entire job it is to know when the hot toys will be available. "It could be in the next shipment." Or it could be the day before Christmas, causing a melee of unparalleled proportions as panicked parents storm the stores for the one gift they think will make their child eternally happy and satisfied.

No, thanks.

Before I go back online and sell my soul to the Amazon.com devil, I decide to try one more tack with my son.

"Tell you what," I say. "Since we just got you a new Game Boy last year, if you really want another one, I'll split it with you."

"What do you mean?" he asks warily.

"I'll pay for half and you pay for half with your allowance money."

He looks aghast. I can see the gears turning, the numbers being subtracted, and the smoke coming out of his ears as he calculates how much of a dent this will make in his life savings. Suddenly, it seems, the Game Boy Advance SP in titanium isn't *that* cool.

Mom, 1; Game Boy, 0.

April Showers Bring May Diets

I'm not a big fan of the winter, and of weather so cold that your nostrils stick together when you inhale. But at least in winter nobody can tell if you gained any weight because you're covered up in thick sweaters and bulky jackets. Then spring rolls around and it's panic time because you know summer is just around the corner and you'll have to put on a bathing suit, and the truth will come out that you did *not* spend every breathing minute at the gym as you said you did, or survive on protein bars but instead ate more than your fair share of Krispy Kremes for about six months running.

I know I'm not alone in this, so at least there is comfort in numbers. I have one friend who's gained and lost enough weight every year to make a whole other person. She thinks that sensible eating is the key to weight loss — for other people. She's tried every new diet known to woman. She's done the Bloomingdales Diet, Scarsdale, and Sugarbusters. She's eaten only beets for one week and only lima beans for the next. Actually, I think that one was called the Disgusting Vegetables Diet. She's taken these mystery herbal pills she ordered online that have since been banned in America after two dozen people grew something like an extra liver from taking them. She owns a Thigh Master, a Butt Buster, and this special cream that is supposed to melt cellulite if she slathers it on her thighs and then wraps them in cellophane. Not only didn't it melt the fat, it actually increased the hair growth on her upper thighs. Now, each summer she has to diet *and* have her legs waxed weekly. Bummer.

Currently she's on a combination of Atkins and South Beach, eats nothing but steak and eggs, and has a cholesterol count so high that Lipitor wants to pay *her* to take their drugs. When I told her I needed to lose weight, she tried to recruit me into her fad diet cult. I'd rather stay inside for the summer than subject myself to a season of lima beans and hairy thighs, so I politely declined.

Still, there was no denying that something needed to be done. The smart thing would have been to get started the day the groundhog poked his head out of the dirt. But there was still Valentine's Day chocolate to be eaten, and it seemed premature to get hysterical when there was a foot of snow on the ground. Now, however, everywhere I looked, people were practically screaming at me to get my soon-to-be-tankini-covered-bottom in gear while I still could. As I passed my health club on the way to the supermarket, I noticed big bold writing on the windows: "Only six more weeks until summer!" This might not officially be true, but it was scary enough to make me dump a couple gallons of Slim Fast into my shopping cart.

Later that night, as I tried on last year's bathing suit, I said to my husband, "Do I look like I gained weight since last summer?"

He looked up at me over the top of his *Sports Illustrated* swimsuit magazine. "Has any husband ever in the history of the world been stupid enough to answer that question?"

"Do I?" I asked again, ignoring his first response.

"Honey, you always look beautiful to me."

"You're not answering my question."

"Hmm, I think it looks like rain," he said, looking out the window.

"Hmmmph!" I stomped out of the room and downstairs to where the kids were watching TV. Kids are always brutally honest, so I decided to model my suit for them.

"Hey, guys, how do you like this bathing suit?"

My daughter glanced over. "You have extra butt hanging out the back," she said and turned back to the TV.

I picked up the phone and called my diet friend.

"Exactly how much thigh hair are we talking about, really?"

Interlude VIII:
The Long Road Home

"Hey, Mom, are we almost home?"

"We just got on the road."

"How much longer?"

"Three hours and 52 minutes."

"*What?* That's soooo long. I'm freakin'!"

"You're freakin'?"

"Yeah. Hey, Mom, do we have any snacks in the car?"

"You ate them all already."

"But I'm so hungry. I'm starving!"

"You're starving? I thought you were freakin'."

"I'm freakin' starving!"

"Do something to take you mind off it."

"There's nothing to do."

"Look out the window."

"At what?"

"See if you can find a moose."

"There are no moose in Vermont."

"Sure there are. Haven't you seen all the Moose Crossing signs?"

"I thought that was a joke."

"No joke."

"Hey, Mom, can we take one of those signs and put it up at home?"

"No."

"Why?"

"Because there are no moose in New Jersey."

"How do you know?"

"Have you ever seen a moose in New Jersey?"

"No. But I've never seen a moose in Vermont, either, so what's the difference?"

"We can't take their signs. They need them so people don't hit the moose."

"I don't think that's a problem."

"Why?"

"Because there are no moose!"

"Just because you haven't seen them doesn't mean there aren't any."

"Then how do you know there aren't any moose in New Jersey?"

(Sigh.) "Can we change the subject?"

"Sure." (Pause.) *"Oh my gosh... I see a moose!"*

"Really? Where???"

"Over there!!!"

"Where? I don't see it!"

"Just kidding."

"That's not funny."

"Yes, it is."

"No. It's not."

"Yes. It is. Hey, Mom, welcome to Massachusetts!"

"What are you talking about?"

"There's a sign that says 'Welcome to Massachusetts.'"

"Yeah, right."

"No, really."

"Are you serious?"

"Totally."

"Shoot! We're going the wrong way. I must have missed the turn-off when I was looking for the stupid moose."

"There *are* no moose."

Quacking Up

Tales from the Beckerman Beach Club, Part 1

"Hey, Mom, look outside," yelled my son one fine May morning. "We've got ducks."

Sure enough, a lovely mallard couple was sitting beside the pool, trying to determine if the water was to their liking, or perhaps hoping a waiter would come by with a couple of spritzers. After awhile they flew off, probably dissuaded by the aroma of chlorine wafting into their bills.

They returned every day for a week without dipping so much as one webbed toe in the water before flying off. Then one day, after surveying the scene, they took the plunge. They swam, they floated, they had an all-around marvelous time. And then they did what ducks do: they shed feathers, and they pooped in the pool.

I was not amused. I ran outside in my jammies, waving my arms and yelling at the ducks to go away. Did I mention it was 6:45 a.m.? I'm sure the neighbors were thrilled.

My young daughter was delighted, though. The next thing I knew she had appeared on the deck with a loaf of potato bread, which she gleefully tore into pieces and tossed in the pool.

"What are you *doing?*" I screamed.

"Feedin' the ducks," she responded.

I suppose I should consider myself lucky that we only had ducks in our pool. In Florida, I hear pool-owners routinely report alligators taking a dip. At least our feathered pool guests wouldn't eat the kids.

Still, I worried that word would get out amongst the duck community about this wonderful new aquatic retreat — a little shy on fish, but pleasantly warm and relaxing. A duck spa, I was not prepared to own. Besides, I think you need a variance for that.

In the grand scheme of things, ducks in the pool are not as bad as, say, friends who routinely invite themselves over for a swim and then lounge about until dinnertime waiting for an invite to stay for pizza or burgers. Or the ones who drop off their children for a swim date and then, on their way out, remind me not to let the kids out of the shallow end because they can't swim. At least I know ducks won't drown.

On the flip side, my human guests don't generally shed feathers in the pool, and the adults, at least, do go in the house to use the bathroom.

Ducks eat grubs, which are in free supply. My friends consume all my potato chips, beer, and soda, which are not.

The ducks would, if so inclined, mate in my pool. My friends, hopefully, would get a room.

Being somewhat generous ducks, they probably would not mind if the people decided to join them for a dip in the pool.

The people, however, might not be quite so thrilled to swim with the ducks.

That being the case... I might let the ducks stay.

Tales from the Beckerman Beach Club, Part 2

Last summer we had a chuckle at two ducks doing the breaststroke in our hot tub. We stopped laughing when they decided to stay. Two ducks for a day is funny. Two ducks for a whole summer is a whole lot of duck poop in my pool.

Eventually they took off for friendlier waters. It might have had something to do with us closing the pool in September, but who knows.

Then one night as I was putting my daughter to bed, I happened to glance outside and saw the duck couple from last summer in the pool. How did I know they were the same? Well, I'm no duck expert, but what are the chances that another male and female mallard would start swimming in our pool?

"Honey!" I yelled downstairs to my husband. "The ducks are back."

"Is that a secret code for something?"

"No, the *ducks!* From last summer. They're in the pool. Actually, the hot tub." Since he's the guy who cleans the pool, he was less happy about this than I. The kids, of course, were thrilled. Why settle for just a dog when you can have two ducks to boot?

And me? Well, you have to understand, I am not a bird person. I had a roommate in college who allowed her cockatiel to fly free around our apartment. Did you know you can't housebreak a cockatiel? There was cockatiel poop everywhere. It even managed to get into my closet. I think even Mr. Blackwell would agree that bird poop on your clothes is a fashion don't.

To add insult to injury, my parking spot in college was right under a lovely maple tree. The birds liked to perch in the maple tree. There wasn't enough washer fluid in the world to tackle that assault.

And then there was my apartment in New York City with a nice fat ledge where the pigeons liked to hang out. Their perch was on the second floor of our duplex, so you can imagine what the window on the first floor underneath it looked like.

My life, in a sense, has been for the birds.

Which brings us to the ducks. The next morning I decided to go to the pet store while the ducks floated leisurely in the pool.

"There are *no fish* in there!" I yelled on my out. They ignored me.

"Don't forget to pick up some birdseed," said my son. I glared at him.

At the pet store, I asked the guy, "How do you get rid of ducks in a pool?"

"Shotgun?" he suggested. I backed out of the store quickly.

I stopped at the hardware store and examined a can of RAID. It didn't say anything about ducks.

When I got home, the ducks were still swimming, and I had to stop my daughter before she could take them another loaf of bread. As I started outside to assess the situation, I tripped over the dog.

The dog! Last year we didn't have a dog. Now, not only did we have a dog, we had a sporting dog, a retriever, specially bred to hunt... *ducks!*

I gave my most evil, sinister, duck-riddance laugh, opened the door, and called softly, "Oh, Riley..."

The dog barked, ducks quacked, feathers flew, and the ducks flew the coop.

Too bad I didn't have a dog when I lived with that damned cockatiel.

Having a Pool Isn't All It's Quacked up to Be

Like the return of the swallows to Capistrano, each spring the same mallard couple returns back to our house to dip their webbed feet in our pool. I don't know where they wintered — probably Palm Beach like my grandparents did — but I imagined them down there playing pinochle with the other snowbirds, saying, "Yes, we have a lovely place up north in New Jersey. It's a natural stone pool with a small waterfall and plenty of worms for me and the Mrs. The chlorine is hell on our feathers, but you can't beat the privacy."

I was actually surprised to see the ducks back again this year after our dog had invaded their tranquility the previous summer. But, once they realized that our retriever, a water dog, was terrified of water, they must have decided that a little barking was worth their exclusive membership in the Beckerman Beach Club.

"The ducks are back," I informed my family at dinner that night. The kids were ecstatic.

"Can we keep them? Do they have ducklings? Can we *keep the ducklings? Can they stay in my room???!!!*"

"No. Maybe. No. No," I responded.

"Can we have them with orange sauce and wild rice?" asked my husband, the comedian.

I shook my head. "I won't pluck our dinner."

"Seriously, honey, you have to get rid of them," he told me. "The feathers will clog the filter." Oh sure, I thought. I'll just put on my official duck-catcher uniform, whip out my trusty de-ducking device, and rid our pool of all uninvited poultry.

"How do you suggest I do that?"

"Call somebody," he said.

"Who?"

"I don't know. The Fish and Game people? The ASPCA? Terminex?"

I checked the Yellow Pages, but there was nothing under pool maintenance or pest control to address our particular problem. I thought back to my younger days watching *Mutual of Omaha's Wild Kingdom*, but Marlon Perkins had never covered this specific issue either.

When the ducks returned the next day, I snuck out to the pool and then ran inside the fence, waving my arms like an idiot and yelling at the top of my lungs. All I can say is, thank God there were no TV cameras hidden in the bushes.

Eventually the ducks took off and I went back inside, confident that I had done the deed. But five minutes later I heard a splash and looked out my back door to see the mallards doing a swan dive into the pool. I looked at the dog sleeping on the rug.

"Where's your pride?" I accused him. "You're a retriever.

You're bred specifically to go in the water and retrieve ducks. I want a refund."

He got up lazily, did a big stretch, and then went to the back door to go out. As he stood on the deck, he suddenly became aware of the ducks in the pool and bolted for the backyard.

I watched as he ran from one end of the pool to the other, barking as the ducks swam back and forth like, well, like ducks in a shooting gallery.

Suddenly one of the ducks rose up and sort of flapped its way across the pool. The dog, worked up to a point of frenzy now, ran forward and took a flying leap into the shallow end.

I was flabbergasted. I completely forgot about the ducks and ran to save the dog, who, having never swam before, would probably sink like a rock and drown. However, as I got to the pool, I saw the dog doggie-paddle to the steps, calmly walk out and shake himself off.

In all the excitement, I hardly noticed that the ducks had flown the coop.

"Congratulations," I said to the dog. "You've brought honor back to your breed." I guess all he needed was the right motivation.

Now I just have to figure out how to keep the dog out of the pool.

Return of the Call of the Wild

"Mom, the ducks are back," my son announced while I was making dinner one night.

"Ha, ha," I said without looking up. It was only April 23, way too early for the annual appearance of the mallard couple who take up temporary residence in our pool every summer.

"No, Mom, I'm serious," he insisted.

I probably would have continued mashing potatoes without hesitation if not for the fact that the dog was barking his way into a well-frothed fit in the family room. Laying down my mashing spoon, I walked out on the deck. Sure enough, there on the diving rock was the Mrs., quacking at me with disgust over, I assume, the fact that we had not yet removed our pool cover.

"Excuse me," I yelled to the duck. "Is it my fault you two decided to head up north early this year?" I noticed her husband was swimming in very, very small circles in the water that had accumulated in the center of the pool cover, but soon he gave up and joined his wife quacking on the rock.

"Like I don't have enough people complaining around here," I mumbled. In a huff I turned around, let the deck door fly open, and watched with satisfaction as the dog barked the ducks back to Boca Raton.

But alas, they stayed. And this year, it seemed, they were a little annoyed. Maybe it was the pool cover. Or maybe they weren't happy that they had arrived during Passover and had to settle for *matzoh* handouts from my daughter, instead of the usual potato bread.

Whatever the reason, every day when they arrived for their mid-morning swim, they stood on the pool deck and quacked. A lot. Then the dog would bark. A lot. Finally I would let the dog out, he'd chase the ducks, they'd fly away, and then ten minutes later the whole thing would start all over again.

Don't think I didn't toy with the idea of getting a school of piranha or a shark. But somehow I thought that might compound the problem. Besides, I don't think we're zoned for man-eating wildlife in my town.

About two weeks into the duck issue, my husband and I went out to dinner.

"How are you doing getting rid of the ducks?" he asked innocently.

"How am *I* doing?" I replied. "When did this become *my* problem? Who appointed *me* official duck-ridder?"

"You are the one who's home all day, honey. It's kind of up to you."

I glowered. "Well, in case you missed the feathers in the pool, the ducks are still here. I can't figure out how to get rid of them, but if the past four summers are any indication, they'll be gone in about two weeks." I paused. "But

I'm still really annoyed."

Smart man that he is, he let the subject drop and signaled the waiter to come over.

"Are you ready to order?" our waiter asked.

My husband studied the menu. "I'll have the steak," he said.

"And you, ma'am?" asked the waiter, turning to me.

I smiled.

"Duck."

The Early-Bird Special

⌐

There's a lot that I look forward to with the arrival of spring: longer days, warmer weather, flowers blooming. But the ducks returning to our pool... eh, not so much.

Last year we thought we had the problem licked. The ducks arrived during Passover so all they got to eat was *matzoh*. They left in a month.

But they must have converted to Judaism over the winter, because this year they returned well in time for the whole eight days of Passover — and they bought a friend. His name is Sy.

Now, Larry, Loretta, and Sy of Boca Raton, Florida, are all hanging out by the pool *kvetching*[1] about how long the flight was, how cold it is up here, and the fact that the pool tarp is still on.

"What is this *mishigas*[2]?" quacked Sy. "You dragged me all the way up here, I'm freezing my tail feathers off, and we can't even swim in the pool? *Oy*, my wings are killing me. Where's that kid with the *matzoh*, anyway?"

To me, obviously, all this just sounded like a whole lot

---

[1] complaining
[2] craziness

of quacking, which was bad enough. But all that quacking made the dog do a whole lot of barking. Soon there was a cacophony of animal noise in my backyard. I decided the time had come for Larry, Loretta, and Sy to check into the Hebrew Home for Aged Ducks or someplace else more hospitable that also, possibly, had a shuffleboard court.

This is when Sy fell into the pool. Not just into the pool, but under pool cover. There had been a gap between the tarp and the edge of the pool, and when Sy tried to fly out, he fell in.

Oops. You want graceful? Get swans in your pool. Ducks... eh, not so much.

From under the tarp I heard splashing and quacking and I realized I was going to have to play Baywatch to make sure Sy didn't become a dead duck.

"What kind of *meshungina*[3] duck gets stuck in a pool?" quacked Loretta and Larry from the deck.

"What kind of *meshungina* ducks swim in a pool???" I yelled at the mallards.

I yanked the tarp back — no easy feat, considering it was loaded with rainwater, leaves, and other winter muck. Then I lay down and hung over the edge of the pool, splashing water at Sy to get him to fly out the hole. Definitely a low point in my suburban life.

Finally my backup arrived. Upon hearing all the noise, the dog charged out of the house, climbed on my back, and barked in Sy's face.

---

[3] crazy

And with that, the duck flew away.

I got up and plucked pebbles from the palms of my hands.

"You're a real *mensch*[4], Riley," I told the dog.

"Just doin' my job," he barked back.

---

[4] good person

Interlude IX:
The First Annual
Lost in Suburbia Awards

Hot on the heels of last week's Emmy Awards, we're getting ready for the First Annual "Lost in Suburbia Awards." We're here at Dunkin' Donuts Stadium, where the air is thick with excitement and the aroma of hazelnut coffee. The parking lot is filling to capacity with minivans and oversized SUVs as nominees and soccer moms, decked out in their GAP finest, are beginning to strut down the red carpet in anticipation of this evening's big event.

Expectations are high tonight for several young actors and actresses who gave outstanding performances in various roles this year. Young Emily Beckerman, a relative newcomer to the performing arts, competes in several categories for her convincing role as a misunderstood child, including Best Actress in a Bedtime Performance for her imaginative portrayal of a young girl who says she can't sleep because her skin is too tight.

Her other nominations include Best Actress in a Homework Performance for her inability to do her assignments because her brain is sore, and Best Actress in a Dinner Performance for her refusal to eat peas because they look like little alien eyeballs.

In an unusual twist this year, Emily Beckerman and her mother, Tracy, are competing against each other in the category of Best Performance in a Domestic Crisis for their dual roles in this years' hit comedy *Help! 500 Crickets Are Loose in the House!*

Another young actor taking center stage is Josh Beckerman, shining in his role in several challenging categories, including Best Actor in a Video Game Performance for arguing that video games qualify as exercise because they work out his thumbs.

A new category this year is the Best Supporting Pet Performance where Riley Beckerman is the favorite for his role in the music video "Dancing in the Wet Concrete Subfloor."

Einstein, the bearded dragon, is in the running for Outstanding Lost Pet in a Performance for his role as a missing lizard who freaks out the housekeeper and causes her to quit. Word has it that Einstein's biggest challenger for the award is a six-foot boa constrictor named George who got lost in an elementary school cafeteria.

Women, children, and reptiles are not the only ones competing this year. Veteran actor Joel Beckerman is up for several awards, including Best Performance by a Beleaguered Husband for his role in the low-budget thriller *My Wife Spent Too Much Money at the Mall.* This is Beckerman's third nomination in this category, having won the award once before for his role in the prequel, *My Wife Spent Too Much Money at Bed, Bath & Beyond.*

Back on the red carpet, Tracy Beckerman has just arrived, looking very sharp in a vintage Old Navy frock with authentic spaghetti-sauce stains on the lapel. She's expected to sweep tonight's awards in the Best Performance in a Plumbing Catastrophe category, Best Performance Crying Her Way out of a Traffic Ticket, and Best Performance in a Remake for *Honey, I Shrunk the Laundry.*

The show is about to begin. To all you actors and actresses, remember, here in suburbia, it's not who you know, but what you drive that matters, and, as always, it's an honor just to be nominated.

Our Wild Kingdom

We're off to Seek the Lizard

You know that thing you can put on your keys so when you press a button on a remote, it beeps so you can find your lost keys?

I'm getting one of those for our lizard.

Yes, it's true, the unthinkable happened. After barely a week in our household, we lost Einstein, the lizard. I'm being extremely generous when I say "we," because I personally had nothing to do with the losing of said lizard. My son had him out for some TV time (Einstein, it seems, also enjoys watching *SpongeBob Squarepants*), and the lizard made a run for it.

I wouldn't be exaggerating if I said I turned the house upside-down looking for him. I was a woman possessed as images danced through my head of little lizard feet scuttling across my face while I slept. I have now seen the frightening underside of my sofa, brushed cobwebs from my face as I climbed through the belly of my coat closet, and determined that overall, my cleaning lady is doing a lousy job of cleaning under my furniture.

In her defense, she took it in stride when I told her to watch where she vacuumed because there was a lizard lost in the house somewhere. She told me firmly that if she found it, not only would she not touch it, she would in all likelihood run screaming from our house never to return, and I would not only be out one pretty expensive baby bearded dragon, but I'd have to hire a new cleaning service as well.

Trying to find a lost lizard that is a mere six inches long is no easy task. At least in the past, when we'd lost our hamsters (are you noticing a trend here?), we didn't have to look at the top of the curtains, under the refrigerator, or in the heating vents. Hamsters don't climb window treatments and typically are too fat to get under appliances and through vents. Moreover, Bob and Ted (the hamsters, may they rest in peace) left "evidence" behind them as they scurried about (kind of like Hansel and Gretel with the breadcrumbs, only much grosser), making it pretty easy to follow the trail to their hiding places.

When I reported the news of the lost lizard, a unified chuckle went up among my friends and family. Supportive lot, they are not. The problem was, they all remember when I lost another pet (no, not Bob and Ted, this was before the hamsters). He was a baby corn snake named Fred that I'd bought on a whim when I lived in an apartment in the city. One night Fred got out of his cage (okay, so maybe I'd left it open a crack) and disappeared into the exposed brick wall that ran the length of one side of my apartment. We never saw him again, although from that day on I never saw another mouse or cockroach in my apartment, either, so that was a bonus.

Anyway, on my hands and knees I went, flashlight in

hand, from 8 p.m. LLT (Lost Lizard Time) to midnight, and then again the next day until that night, when my computer crashed. I got on the floor to reboot the modem, only to find Einstein resting comfortably amid the dusty cables. Lucky for him, the cleaning lady doesn't clean under there, either.

This is one lucky lizard. For a day, he managed to avoid being eaten by a dog, sucked up by a vacuum cleaner, or unceremoniously squished by human feet.

Truly, I'm grateful, and no, I'm not sorry we got the lizard.

If my son had had his way, I might have been looking for a tarantula.

A Cricket in Queen Tracy's Court

One morning I woke not to the usual blaring of my alarm clock, but to the sound of crickets chirping.

I thought maybe I was dreaming about camping. But then I remembered that I am a primadonna and I don't go camping because, among other reasons, I don't like to listen to crickets chirping. No, I wasn't dreaming. Much to my dismay, I realized that the chirping was coming from someplace very near, like, oh, um, right inside my bedroom.

"Josh!" I yelled. My son appeared at my door.

"Do you, the owner of the lizard that eats crickets, have any idea why I am hearing crickets in my bedroom?" He grinned. Apparently my near-hysteria was high on the list of things boys find funny.

"Um, I was feeding Einstein last night and I think a few crickets might have escaped," he admitted.

"You *think?*"

"Well, actually, I accidentally knocked the whole cricket tank over. But I thought I caught them all." His eyes flicked around my bedroom as the chirping started again.

"That's just great," I huffed. "They're probably all in the vents now where they will lie in wait until we go to sleep and then they will crawl out and walk across my face."

I shivered. He snickered.

"How do you suppose we're going to catch them?" I asked him.

"We can let Einstein loose to find them," he said. In my not-so-distant memory I recalled the last time my son had let his lizard loose. Einstein had suddenly discovered he could run really fast on the wood floors and for 24 hours, he was a lizard on the lam. Surprisingly, it was the cleaning lady who found the lizard. Not so surprisingly, the cleaning lady then quit.

"Forget it. I just hired a new cleaning service. I'm not going through that again."

"No, Mom, it's okay. If we lose Einstein, we can send the dog to find him!"

"Probably not a good idea," I said.

"Why?"

"Here's the food chain," I explained. "The lizard eats the crickets. The dog eats the lizard."

"Oh."

I sent my son off to get ready for school and tiptoed around my bedroom, praying I wouldn't feel anything crunch under my bare feet. I tried to put the crickets out my mind — no easy feat with all that chirping going on. Finally, I tried whistling a tune to distract myself until I realized I was whistling along with the beat of the chirping.

Now, living things in nature generally don't bother me when they're outside where they belong. I can bait a hook and catch a frog with the best of them. But when something gets in the house, I suddenly become one of those women who jumps up on chairs and shrieks. It's the element of surprise. I just don't do well with things that suddenly pop out of closets and drawers and jump on me... whether they are crawly, furry, or children.

Anyway, back at Bug Central, I got busy with breakfast, dropped off the kids, and ran some errands, and by the time I got home I had forgotten all about the wayward crickets. So I was completely unprepared when I walked through the dining room and an enormous cricket hopped into my path. I shrieked and jumped out of the way, and then the dog, hot on my heels, lunged forward and devoured the cricket.

It may not be the right order in the food chain, but it got the job done.

Don't Forget to Pack the Lizard

Most people take vacations as a break from work, school, and laundry. Personally, I find I need a vacation from getting ready to go on vacation. But the hardest part about going away is *not* the getting-everything-I-need part, or the packing-everything-up part, or holding the mail, or stopping the newspapers, or any of the other hundred little things I have to do to close up my house for ten days. No, for me, the biggest pain is finding someone to come in and feed my son's lizard while we're away.

When I complain about this to my friends, they say, "Why don't you just board him, like your dog?" That would be a good solution — if I were a weightlifter, because the lizard's in a 40-gallon tank and I would hate to start my vacation with a herniated disc. Then my friends say, "Why don't you just leave a ton of food in his tank?" This, too, would be a good solution, if the lizard weren't a pig who would eat a week's worth of crickets in one fell swoop and then throw them up, like my kids do when I give them a bag of candy and tell them to have just a few pieces.

It's one thing to be the mother of the kid with the lizard, scooping a dozen live crickets out of a container, into a plastic bag with vitamin powder, and then into the lizard tank.

It's quite another to ask someone else to do it. I thought about paying the neighbor's kid to come over and do it, because I'm fairly certain that a 12-year-old boy would have no problem handling a veritable plague of disgusting bugs. However, I was also fairly certain that for every cricket he caught, ten more would escape into the crevices of my home, only to reappear later on my face when I was sleeping, or in the bathroom when my mother visited, or on the head of the third new cleaning lady who still doesn't even know about the lizard.

Since we're still catching errant crickets from the last cricket jailbreak, maybe the solution would be to just set the lizard free and let him feed off the fat of the land, so to speak. Plus, with the dog away, the lizard could patrol the house and keep away any intruders. I know if I went to rob a house and then a lizard the length of my arm came around the corner, hissing and blowing up his beard, I wouldn't stick around to find out if he only ate crickets.

However, if for some reason we were unable to locate him when we got home, I think my visiting mother would find it infinitely more shocking to have a lizard appear in the bathroom rather than a little cricket.

Ultimately I convinced my college-aged, oh-so-responsible babysitter to come in and feed the reptile. I left her the key, the crickets, and some very explicit instructions. When we arrived home ten days later, I immediately went to my son's room. All the crickets were gone and the lizard looked fat and happy — or at least fat and alive.

"Success," I announced to my husband, gesturing to

the tank as he walked into the room.

But before he could congratulate me, we heard my daughter scream from the floor below.

"Mommy, come here quick! There's crickets in the bathroom!!"

I looked at my husband and then picked up the phone.

"I'd better warn my mother."

...And Chinchilla Makes Three

I used to think my friends who had more than two kids were crazy. All those meals to make — all that mess — all that noise! No, thank you. I kept my brood at a comfortable, manageable two. And then we got a dog. And then we got a lizard. And now, the latest addition to the Beckerman Zoo: a chinchilla. Suddenly I realized that when my friends' children have all grown up and moved away, I will still have a lizard and a chinchilla to take care of. Who's the crazy one?

"You got a what?" asked my mother.

"A chinchilla," I said. "It's cute. It's cuddly."

"It's a rodent," she said. "Or a coat. Why in the world would you get one?"

"Emily asked for a pet for her birthday."

"Did it ever occur to you to say no?"

I recalled the four dogs, five cats, various turtles and fish, and the snake (for five minutes) we had when I was growing up and decided she wasn't the best person to lecture me.

I have to admit, the dog was my idea. However, I had been under the mistaken impression that in addition to being a nice companion, having a dog would teach my kids some responsibility. Needless to say, I was the one who ended up doing the feeding, walking, and cleaning up, after which I firmly decided that we would remain a one-pet family.

Then my son decided he wanted a lizard, and my husband convinced me that we should encourage my son's interests. But with the scales of sibling equality unbalanced, I was hardly surprised when my daughter said she wanted her own pet. Which leads us to our current menagerie. Honestly, I have nothing against pets. But three pets means three different "meals" to make every day, and three different places to board the pets when we go out of town. At least with my kids, I can board them both at their grandparents' house.

Three pets means three times the chances that one of them will escape and get lost in the house (although it would be pretty easy to find the dog), bite and/or slobber on a guest, or be stupid enough to bark at a skunk (guess who).

Of course, three pets also means three times the material for my columns.

Column or no column, after I saw how the chinchilla delighted in chucking his bedding onto the floor of my daughter's bedroom, I made an announcement to the world that the Beckerman Zoo was officially closed to new inhabitants.

Then my son's birthday arrived. In the aftermath of his 25-friend birthday-party extravaganza, he sat on the floor tearing the wrapping paper off his deluge of gifts. When he got to the final item, he held it up for inspection.

"What's this?" he asked, examining the jar. His sister approached and read the label.

"Grow a frog," she announced. "Oh, cool. They send

you a baby tadpole and you can grow it into a real frog."

I groaned. "Who gave you that gift?"

"The same kid who gave me the fish tank last year." As the dog started shredding the discarded wrapping paper, I mentally marked the frog friend off next year's guest list.

"Hey, doesn't he have a birthday coming up soon, too?" I asked my son.

"Yeah."

"I wonder if he'd like a snake…"

All Aboard the Beckerman Bus

As a suburban mom, I'd always expected that in addition to doing laundry, making meals, and butting heads over homework, there would be a fair amount of taxi driving. What I didn't count on was that my chauffeuring duties would include not only my kids and their friends, but also the assorted pets in my household.

Ignorant me. I had always thought our dog, lizard, and chinchilla would just hang out at home in their cages or tanks, or clinging to the living room drapes when they escaped from their cages and tanks. But no, it seemed our animals also had extracurricular activities that necessitated a certain amount of driving and swearing on my part.

I realized all this one day as I was preparing to go out of town on a week's vacation. Our dog, Riley, had an appointment at the doggie salon for a much-needed grooming. But as the Beckerman bus was pulling out of the driveway, my son informed me that his lizard was scheduled to make a guest appearance at the elementary school that day.

"Can't we reschedule Einstein?" I begged my son. "It took me two weeks to get Riley this grooming appointment, which he needs before he goes to the kennel."

"No, Mom," he said impatiently. "I had to get double

special top-security clearance for an exotic animal to come to the school, today only!" I imagined the superintendent of schools and my son's principal playing rock, paper, scissors to decide if the lizard could get a one-day grade-school visa.

"Well, the dog's appointment is at 10:00, he has to get to the boarders' by 3:30 and the lizard isn't due at the school until 2:00. So I guess I can do it all," I said. Of course, I had a frightening list of things to do before we left town, but I was foolishly confident that I could make it all work without imploding.

Giddy with my multitasking capabilities, I dropped the dog off at the groomer's and swung by my house to pick up the dry-cleaning and feed Henry, the chinchilla. However, when I gazed into the chinchilla mansion, I noticed that Henry looked a little listless — quite a feat for a nocturnal animal in the afternoon. Since I didn't want to come home from vacation to a dead chinchilla, I decided to run him over to the vet to get him checked out. The problem was, they didn't have an appointment until 1.

Here's where things got hairy.

1:00 p.m.: I bring the chinchilla to the vet. While there, I get a call from the groomer that the dog is ready.

1:45 p.m.: I throw the chinchilla back in the car and run home to get the lizard.

1:55 p.m.: No time to drop off the chinchilla. I scoop up the lizard, throw him in a pet carrier, and bring him to school. The chinchilla is making a weird noise. I think he wants off the bus.

2:10 p.m.: Back to the groomer's to pick up the dog.

Still have the chinchilla in the car, and now the dog.

2:45 p.m.: No time to drop off the chinchilla and the dog. Go back to the school to get the lizard and the kids.

3:10 p.m.: No time to drop off the lizard and the chinchilla. Stop at the pet shop to get more dog food for the kennel and crickets for the lizard.

I now have two kids, a dog, a lizard, a chinchilla, and 60 crickets in the car. I pray I don't get stopped by a cop for anything because there is no way I could explain this scenario without being subjected to a breathalyzer.

3:30 p.m.: I drop the dog off at the kennel, the kids at their after-school activities, and the lizard, the chinchilla, and the crickets back at the house.

Later that night, when my husband got home, I lay prone on the couch.

"How was your day, honey?" he asked.

I glared at him. "Ruff."

Interlude X:
A Lesson in Homework

"Hey, pussycat, it's time to turn off the TV and do your social studies homework."

"Five more minutes."

"You said that five minutes ago."

"But Mom, this is the best part of the show."

"It was the best part five minutes ago. Go!"

"The homework is stupid."

"It's not stupid. It helps you understand what you learned in school."

"I already understand what we learned in the school. *'We the people, in order to form a more perfect union...'*"

"GO!"

"It's my homework. Don't I have any say?"

"No."

"Can we vote on it?"

"No."

"I thought this was a free country!"

"The *country* is free, but this *house* is a dictatorship and I'm the ruler."

"That's not fair."

"Hey, at least in this regime, you get dessert after you finish your homework."

"Can I have ice cream?"

"No, you already had ice cream today."

"When I'm president, I'm going to outlaw homework and allow ice cream twice a day."

"You won't get to be president unless you do your homework."

"I bet the president can have ice cream twice in one day."

"I'll ask his mother."

"Really?"

"No. Now quit stalling."

"I'm not stalling. I'm invoking my First Amendment right."

"Your First Amendment right?"

"Yes."

"Do you know what that is?"

"Yes. Freedom of speech."

"How old are you?"

"Nine."

"You're right. You don't need to do the homework."

It's All about Me

The French Connection

I'm having an affair.

My kids know, of course, because they're usually with me when it happens.

I know it's wrong, but no matter how many promises I make to myself, I am unable to stop it. Much as I hate to admit it, I'm in love... with McDonald's french fries.

It didn't have to be McDonald's. It could just as easily have been Wendy's or Burger King. McDonald's just happens to be closer to my house — and when you're having an affair, proximity is everything.

I truly loathe my weakness. I know it's bad for my relationship with my thighs, but I can't seem to help myself. I tried going cold turkey, but that didn't work. I thought maybe if I brought it out into the open, it would help me to quit. But my friends were less than supportive.

"Ugh. How can you eat that stuff?" asked my friend Dana. "It's so bad for you."

"I know, I know." I agreed. "But it tastes so good."

"Yeah, it does," said Dana longingly. She, too, has done battle with her french fry demons.

Finally, after much soul-searching and weight gain, I decide to come clean to my husband. One night after a healthy dinner of tofu-and-vegetable stir-fry, I faced him.

"Honey, I have a confession to make," I began. He looked at me, his eyes filled with love and trust.

"I've been eating french fries," I admitted. I was so ashamed. But he reached across the table and took my hand.

"I know."

"How did you know?" I asked incredulously. I thought I had been so diligent about hiding the evidence.

"There was salt on the dashboard in the car. And I could smell the grease."

I buried my head in my arms. "I thought I'd gotten over this. The health club. The Atkins diet. But after the kids were born... it was so hard to stay away."

"I understand," he said. "It happens to a lot of people. If not french fries, maybe Twinkies. You need some help. It's nothing to be ashamed of."

I thought about all those nights sneaking around... eating in the car... rationalizing to myself, "They're just potatoes. Potatoes are good for you. It's not like I'm eating chocolate, for goodness sake."

But the truth was, they weren't *just* potatoes. They were *fried* potatoes. And I had made a promise to myself and my husband on my wedding day that, like caffeine, my fried-food days were behind me. Unfortunately, it wasn't something I could just turn off. It was a constant battle.

However, once I got past the shame, I was able to look at the whole affair more honestly and objectively.

"French fries smell good and they taste good and they make me feel good when I eat them, gosh darnit!"

"But how do you feel *after* you eat them?" asked a reformed french fry eater, who shall remain anonymous.

"I don't feel so good about myself," I admitted.

"That's good. That's the first step in giving up the fries," she said.

I've now been french fry-free for almost two months. Some days I drive past McDonald's and I feel a familiar twinge. But then I get home, I take out my swimsuit, and I feel good about how far I've come.

Now I'm eating baked potatoes. It's not quite the same, but someday, with some sour cream perhaps, I hope to break the french fry habit for good.

Maybe.

Hair Today, Gone Tomorrow

As I was approaching the cash machine, a man walked up at the same time. I waved my hand to let him pass, but he waved back and said, "Ladies first."

"Oh, how nice," I said with surprise. "I haven't heard that for awhile."

"Maybe if you grew your hair a little longer you'd hear it more often," he said seriously.

I was so shocked by this comment that I was rendered virtually speechless. In my car five minutes later, I came up with all the snappy comebacks I wished I'd said five minutes earlier:

"Actually I'm in the middle of a sex change, and I want to keep my hair short until the change is complete."

Or, "Well, this is as much as it's grown back since I finished chemotherapy."

Or perhaps, "I understand only men with male-pattern baldness are threatened by women with short hair."

But of course, at the time, I said nothing. Should I care what a total stranger thought about the length of my hair? Of course not. Yet it really dug under my skin.

I know that I am, with my short spiky hair, unique in the 'burbs. As I peruse the stores at the mall, I'm well aware of the fact that most of the other women there are not as closely shorn as I. Not even close.

However, I've always kind of reveled in my uniqueness. I like the fact that while many women seem to view their hair as a necessary accessory to their femininity, I do not. I love how quickly I can get ready in the morning without being a slave to the blow dryer. And I love when my daughter runs her fingers through my hair and says, "I like your spiky hair, Mommy."

Instead of sending a message to men that my hair is there to please them, I feel I'm sending a message to my daughter that it's wonderful to be different.

If my husband were one of those guys who needed their wives to have long, flowing hair, my crew cut could present a problem. But when I showed up at home a week after our honeymoon with ten fewer inches of hair, he took it in stride.

"Wow, you cut your hair," he remarked. "It looks nice. I like the contrast between the womanly body and the boyish haircut."

This is one of the reasons why I love this man.

Still, for a while I wondered if other women felt that with my short hair, I might be the enemy — a turncoat of my gender, defying the uttermost symbol of our womanliness. But then, several days after the ATM incident, I walked into my local Dunkin' Donuts to get an iced coffee. The woman behind the counter smiled at me.

"You look different," I said to her, not quite able to identify the change in her appearance.

"I always wanted short hair," she replied. She was an Asian woman who used to have cascades of shiny black hair. "After I saw your haircut, I decided to cut mine, too." I then realized she was sporting my short, spiky 'do.

"It looks great on you," I told her. It really did. The short hair brought out her big eyes and the striking cheekbones that had been hidden behind all the hair.

"I know. I love it." She beamed at me. "Thank you."

"No problem," I responded. "And by the way, if any guy makes any rude comments to you about the length of your hair, here are a couple of responses you can give him…"

Bite Me

When I went for oral surgery last spring, the doctor told me he could only do one half of my mouth that day or I wouldn't be able to eat for two weeks. Considering it was almost bathing suit season, I didn't think that was necessarily a bad thing. But he convinced me otherwise, and told me if I was really gung-ho to get it all done, I could come back in a month or so to finish the job. The problem with oral surgery, though, is that after you've gone through it once, it would take a team of wild horses to drag you in there to do it again.

But six months later, when the teeth on the other side of my mouth got so sensitive that even eating plain spaghetti left me in pain, I decided I had to bite the periodontal bullet and go back in the chair.

Let me tell you, there's nothing like having work done on your mouth to make you appreciate little everyday pains like childbirth. The surgery itself was no big deal. The dentist gave me so much novocaine that even my left eyebrow went numb. When the drugs wore off eight hours later and I stopped feeling like my lip was hanging down to my collarbone, and all the drool on my chin had dried up, the throb set in.

Contrary to popular belief, Tylenol does not dull the pain. Advil does not dull the pain. According to my father, the only thing that works is getting hit over the head with a two-by-four. It doesn't lessen the pain in your mouth, but the pain in your head is a good distraction.

My husband and kids were supportive. My husband booked a flight to L.A. and went on a business trip the day of my surgery. I don't blame him. I didn't really want to be around me, either. He did, however, send me a lovely bouquet of roses with wishes for a speedy recovery, which translated to: By the time I return from my trip, you'd better be on the mend.

The kids helped out by answering the phone for me.

"I'm sorry, my mom can't come to the phone," said my daughter. "Her gums are swollen and bleeding and she's a miserable excuse for a human being right now."

At some point, I decided the only thing to do was go to sleep. My mouth had other plans. While my eyes said, "Okay, we're going to sleep now," my mouth said, "Arggh, who can sleep with all this throbbing?" So with an ice pack affixed to my jaw, I stayed up and watched the movies that are so bad they have to run them at three in the morning.

The next day, I not only had a golf ball on the side of my face, I had some very attractive bags under my eyes to boot. All this continued for several more days until I was convinced that a full set of dentures would be a more agreeable alternative. Finally, sick of sitting home with ice on my face, I decided to do the one thing I knew would make me feel better.

Go shopping.

While I was waiting in the checkout line at the store, a very pregnant woman with an infant and four small children got in line behind me. The kids were all yelling and fighting with each other and the mother looked completely fed up. I realized then that my misery would be pretty much over in a week.

She still had 18 years to go.

Real Women Don't Wear Tankinis

This winter, I worked hard to drop a few pounds so that when spring arrived, I wouldn't have to face my annual swimwear terror attack.

Honestly, I find shark-infested waters less scary than trying on bathing suits. Bungee jumping? Piece of cake. Wrestling alligators? Not a problem. Standing half-naked in front of a three-way mirror when I know the security people watching those hidden video cameras are snickering at my cellulite? Nightmare.

With my clothes fitting a little less snugly this year, I was optimistic that I could go bathing-suit shopping without hurling my half-filled Starbucks Frappuccino at the three-way mirror.

Confident that I was tankini-ready, I went to the store and tried on bathing suits two sizes smaller than last year. I was shocked to discover that I still hated how I looked. After trying on several dozen suits, I went back into the store and stood glaring at the racks. After awhile, a teeny-tiny salesgirl approached me.

"Can I help you?" she asked.

Not unless you can miraculously turn these bathing suits into something that will actually look good on me, I thought.

"Well, uh, I'm looking for a bathing suit," I said, stating the obvious.

"How about this one?" she asked as she pulled out something even my grandmother wouldn't have been caught dead wearing at the pool in her retirement community. The thing had more material than my trench coat.

"It's a little old for me, don't you think?" I asked.

"Well, once we're past a certain age, those tiny bikinis just don't flatter us, don't you think?"

What was this "us" stuff? She looked about 22. Besides, I didn't think I was past that "certain age" quite yet. Maybe the fact that I had some smile lines meant to her that I was ready for a bathing suit with an attached skirt and its own breasts, but I begged to differ.

"I was actually looking for a tankini," I told her.

"Hmmm. You know, tankinis are not for everyone. They can actually make your hips look *bigger*." She said this loudly enough to ensure that everyone in the bathing suit department now realized that my hips would look bigger in a tankini.

"I... want... a... tankini!" I said through gritted teeth.

"Well, here's one with a matching sarong. It's nice and long so you can tie it up all the way around your neck and let it drape down like a dress." She modeled the makeshift muumuu on her size-two body for me.

I decided then and there that if I wanted to feel bad about my body, I could do it all by myself, thank you very much.

"You know, thanks, but I think I'll just keep looking on my own," I said and turned back to the tankinis.

"Okay," she said cheerfully. "But you might have better luck over there." She pointed to the section of suck-me-in Miracle Suits, which promise to make you look ten pounds thinner instantly. I gave her the look of death.

"By the way," she said brightly, "When you're ready to buy one, let the cashier know that Katie helped you!"

Fat chance.

But Enough about Me...
Let's Talk about Me

Ever since I heard a story on the news about a cloned baby, I've been wondering if, given the opportunity, I would want to be cloned. Not to delve into the realm of the ethical and political, because this is certainly not that kind of book, but I think there would be certain advantages to having two of me around.

Of course, I wouldn't want to have to start with a mini-me baby. No, give me a fully grown me, and the possibilities are endless. Although I'm not sure my husband would want two of me around to nag him to take out the garbage, hog the bed covers, and snore in stereo, I can't help but wonder about the efficiency of the whole idea. While Original Me is cooking dinner and doing the laundry, Other Me could make the beds and help with homework. Wait a minute... Original Me does all those things at the same time already. Okay. Scratch that. My children would always get my full, undivided attention, even when I'm locked up in my office working. I could dote on my husband when he gets home from work at night and simultaneously be alone with the Sunday *Times* crossword puzzle. I could go with my husband to see an action film or sci-fi movie while also seeing the chick-flick I know he would hate.

Having another me around would be better than having a nanny or an assistant, because everything would get done exactly the way I want it, when I want it, without any explanation, instruction, or assistance. And when one of me screwed up, I wouldn't have to feel bad about it, because I'd know the other me would, and why should we both feel lousy?

Other Me could politely return all the day's phone calls while Original Me, who abhors yakking on the phone at night, could cuddle up with my husband on the couch and watch TV. Other Me could also go to all the PTA meetings, wait in line at the DMV, and do the food shopping, because unlike my husband, Other Me knows that when I write "soda" on the shopping list, I mean Diet Coke, not Diet Pepsi.

On the flip side, I wouldn't have any excuses for not going to the gym, not being able to pick up my husband's dry-cleaning, not having an elegant meal prepared every night, not getting the kids to school on time, or failing to do any of the other things that don't get done because I'm too busy doing something else.

That would be a bummer.

And what if Other Me was a superior cook, a more attentive wife, a more fun mom, and an all-around better me? Would I make me look bad? Would everyone prefer to have Other Me around instead of Original Me?

If the other me really were my clone, not only would I be as efficient as I am, I would also share all my negative traits.

How would my family feel if there were two of us leaving half-empty coffee cups in the car? Two of us moaning about cramps once a month? Two mes flipping out when the dog got into the garbage? It's not a pretty picture.

Perhaps the answer is not to have a clone to handle the overflow of everything I have to accomplish in a day, but rather, not have so much to handle in a day. If I made my to-do list a little more do-able, I would probably feel better about everything I did get done and not focus on the long list of things I couldn't humanly get to.

Two of me might be nice in theory, but in reality I think one of me with a bit more breathing room could accomplish the same thing.

Still, if there were two of me, I could write twice as many columns about pointless theoretical musings.

Reason enough to stick with the original.

Just Sittin' Around
Eating Bonbons

There's this one line on every form I have to fill out that always makes me stop and think: Occupation. Of course I have one, but I don't get compensated financially for it, so I never know if I should just leave it blank or come up with some pithy title for what I do. "Housewife" never felt right to me because, after all, I'm not married to my house, and "Stay-at-Home Mom" just seems too lame. I mean, women who have full-time careers don't write "Working Mom," right? No, they have a title for exactly what I do.

"Woman Who Folds the Socks" lacks that certain *je ne sais quoi*, and doesn't even begin to cover the half of it, anyway. I suppose I could write, "Oh, I don't really do anything. I just sit around eating bonbons all day," which is how I feel when my husband tells me, "We need more milk, could you pick up the dry-cleaning, I'm out of clean underwear, and by the way, what did you do all day, honey?"

I think the kids think of me as the "Human Snack Dispenser," because they don't really address me except when they're in desperate need of a Fruit Roll-Up. I'm sure the dog, if he could speak, would label me "Lady Who Feeds Me and Cleans up My Poop Every Day."

If I came up with a title that really described how I feel most days, it would be something like "Supermom," "Wonder Woman," or "Multi-Tasker Extraordinaire." Then again, there are some days where "Too Tired to Get out of Bed" would be more accurate. Sitting around eating bon-bons all day must wear me out.

Then there's the line on the form where they ask who's the "Head of Household," which is another ambiguous question. I certainly *feel* like the head of the household and am prepared to write in my name until I realize they mean the person who earns the money, which is most definitely *not* me. You certainly wouldn't think of your housekeeper/nanny as the head of the household, yet isn't she the one who keeps things running all day, and in the absence of that person, wouldn't that be me? I know this is true, because our life insurance policy only covers me for the replacement cost of a cleaning person and childcare. (On the upside, I know my husband probably won't have me bumped off to collect the insurance money.)

Coming up with a job title is further complicated by the next question on the form: Employer. That's a toughie. If I'm home taking care of the kids, are they my employer? After all, I am there to meet their needs for the good of the company, even if it's just to provide them with Fruit Roll-Ups (there are no small jobs, only small people). My husband provides me with the money to meet our household expenses, so maybe that makes him my employer, although I'd like to see him try to fire me or give me a bad review. Since I don't get any sick days or personal days or vacation days, I don't think I'm really employed at all. If so, the employee benefits at this company stink.

However, I suppose the personal benefits I enjoy really can't be found at any traditional job. Sure, I don't get paid in cash. But I do get paid in hugs and kisses and finger-paintings that say "You are the best mommy in the whole world!" I've had bosses in the real world who never said boo about my job performance, yet my husband consistently tells me what a great job I'm doing with the kids. And the dog, well. I'm sure he's happy to be fed by *someone*.

Although my college degree is in television theory (yes, there is one), writing, and production, I have life experience in early childhood development, child psychology, education, nursing, residential management, and hordes more specialties. In reality, there's no one who could pay me enough for all of that I'm actually qualified to do.

Still, if I had to boil it all down, I guess "Mommy" would just about cover it. It may not be the highest-earning career, but it's certainly the most valuable one… especially to my employers.

Epilogue:
Step Away from the Minivan with Your Hands Up

"Hello?

"Is this Tracy Beckerman?"

"Who's calling, please?"

"Mrs. Beckerman, this is the suburban police. We received a report of a probable one-nine-two in your area."

"One-nine-two? What's that?"

"Failure to drive a minivan in the suburbs. Do you own a minivan, ma'am?"

"No, officer, I do not."

"Mrs. Beckerman, are you aware that it is compulsory for any family of four or more residing in an area of suburban sprawl, strip malls, and Dunkin' Donuts to be in possession of an oversized, gas-guzzling vehicle?"

"But I do drive an SUV, officer."

"Is it a Suburban, Expedition, or other massive vehicle that's impossible to parallel park and has lousy fuel economy?"

"Uh, no, officer."

"Does your vehicle at least have a third-row option, ma'am?"

"No."

"Then it doesn't meet maximum vehicular requirements for your residential zone."

"But officer, wait, we are looking at the new Honda Pilot right now, which has optional seating for eight and only gets 17 miles per gallon. Oh, and we plan to *lease* it!"

"I'm sorry, ma'am, but that simply doesn't cut it."

"Who turned me in? Was it my neighbor? You know, she doesn't have a minivan either. Or was it the president of the PTA? She drives a Volvo station wagon and it doesn't even have a rear bench!"

"We know all about them, Mrs. Beckerman. Still. I'm afraid I'm going to have to cite you for failure to yield to suburbanization."

"But officer, I'm a soccer mom, we own a Playstation 3, and except for really hot days I almost always get dressed up to go to the mall. We *are* suburbanized!"

"Mrs. Beckerman, if you're intent on blending in here, I strongly suggest you consider leasing a Ford Windstar, endorsing voter apathy, and accepting credit card debt as a way of life. In the meantime, I'm going to write you a warning and recommend that you visit your local Ford dealer to hear about their 0% financing on all minivan models."

"Hang on a second. You're no police officer. You're a telephone marketer! I should have known — it's dinnertime."

"No, ma'am. I'm not a marketer. However, if you would like to make a contribution to the Police Benevolent Association…"

"Officer, are you trying to bribe me?"

"How about the Police Athletic League?"

"Would that get me out of the ticket?"

"No. But we'll send you a really nice sticker for your car."

About the Author

Tracy Beckerman has been a columnist since 2001 with the weekly *Independent Press* newspaper in New Jersey. Her column, LOST IN SUBURBIA®, is carried in 50 other newspapers, including the *Hunterdon County Democrat,* the largest paid weekly newspaper in New Jersey, as well as several other newspapers in the NJN Publishing chain. LOST IN SUBURBIA® is also carried by the community papers of the North Jersey Media Group, reaching more than half a million readers each week.

In addition to her column, Beckerman has written for the *New Jersey Jewish News,* and for two years wrote the bimonthly cover story for the Home and Garden section of New Jersey's largest daily newspaper, *The Star-Ledger.*

Before her foray into journalism, Beckerman spent ten years as a writer and producer in the television industry, managing the advertising and promotion department at WCBS-TV New York, and creating award-winning TV and radio scripts for such clients as Lifetime Television, WCBS-TV, CBS, and NBC. Her numerous honors for writing include a prestigious Writer's Guild of America award, a Clio, an International Film and Television award, and a New York Emmy. She has been selected as a 2007 Humor Writer of the Month by the Erma Bombeck Writer's Workshop, as well as a semi-finalist in the 2005–2006 HumorPress.com "America's Funniest Writer" contest.

She is a member of the National Society of Newspaper Columnists.

Tracy Beckerman is married to a very understanding guy. They have two children and live in New Providence, New Jersey, where she writes, does battle with woodchucks, and avoids, at all costs, driving a minivan.

CPSIA information can be obtained
at www.ICGtesting.com
Printed in the USA
BVOW08s0919061117
499662BV00001B/176/P